D1563314

ONE-ON-ONE:
ONE HUNDRED DAYS WITH JESUS

BARB PEIL

With deep gratitude to each of my Bible teachers,
whose life's best and lasting lesson is showing me Jesus
Ed Peil, Chuck Emert, Chuck Swindoll, J. Vernon McGee,
Jim Lytle, Michael Card, Reg Grant, Rick Houk, Ron Allen.

To you

It's all about Jesus—that's why it works. I was deeply impacted in my personal walk with God this year by this intentional and long look at Jesus, my Savior. Brainstorming each day's piece, I asked the Lord to show me a specific aspect of His character or mission or heart that I could share with you.

The last line, on the last page, sums it up well.

May nothing be more precious to you than Jesus.

If this book stirs that kind of affection and commitment in your heart, then its mission is accomplished.

READ THIS FIRST

Everything good in your life with God happens because of your relationship with Jesus Christ. He is the center—the heart and soul of your life. Twice every year, we pause and consider Jesus' time on earth. We celebrate Christmas, when He came to live with us and remember Easter, when He died for us. A few days later, He conquered death itself and came back to life.

Now, in these snapshots from Jesus' life, see His story from the perspective of those He touched. Look with your heart and your imagination at these 100 snapshots of Jesus. Put them together to discover who He is.

One on One with Jesus will help you better imagine what was going on in those true and familiar stories you've read in the Bible. Begin at the start of the Christmas season and every day through the month of December, meet people from Jesus' backstory. Next, walk with Him into the new year and discover Him in His ministry years. And finally, as Easter approaches, come in from the fringes of the crowd and follow Him on the way to the Cross.

Be the one who moves in so tight that you get the dust off His feet on your sandals.

Be the one He restores from the broken pieces of your past.

Be the one who finally finds the one she's looked for, waited for her whole life.

But even in this crowd of followers, know He loves you as if you were the only one.

Come spend 100 days, one on one with Jesus.

Note: Each day we will explore Jesus' interaction and impact on key people through dramatized accounts based on Scripture. Using all the facts we have, we then use our informed imagination to picture how these events and relationships could have unfolded during Jesus' lifetime on earth. Always read the Bible passage included to complete the authentic occasion and discover what God wants to show you. Not all these events are recorded in Scripture, but are all drawn imaginatively from the question, *what would it be like to walk and talk with Jesus, one on one?*

PART 1
ONE ON ONE WITH JESUS
– IN HIS ADVENT

In the year before Jesus Christ arrived on earth, His backstory was being written in the lives of a handful of people living in northern Israel at the turn of the calendar—real people living mostly insignificant lives. All that changed when God picked them to play a part in history's greatest story. Same as when He invites us into His story . . .

For the next 30 days, take a fresh look at a story you think you already know. Meet the people in Jesus' backstory one on one and you might be surprised how much they remind you of people you know, maybe even yourself.

PART 1
One on One with Jesus – in His Advent

DAY 1

The Year Before

A look at Jesus' backstory

In the beginning was the Word, and the Word was with God, and the Word was God. He was in the beginning with God. All things were made through him, and without him was not any thing made that was made. In him was life, and the life was the light of men. The light shines in the darkness, and the darkness has not overcome it. John 1:1-5

Everyone you meet has a fascinating backstory. Just ask them about it. *Where did you grow up? Who most influenced you? What factors shaped your path? What's important to you? What do you love?*

In the year before Jesus Christ arrived on earth, His backstory was being written in the lives of a handful of people living in northern Israel at the turn of the calendar. Real people living mostly insignificant lives. All that changed when God picked them to play a part in the greatest story in history. Same as when He invites us into His story . . .

1

For the next 30 days, take a fresh look at a story you think you already know. Meet the people in Jesus' backstory one on one and you might be surprised how much they remind you of people you know, maybe even yourself.

We'll start with a peek into what could have been happening in heaven a year before Jesus was born. Then if that's not crazy enough, we'll be there when the glory of heaven comes to earth.

Why take such a journey?

The Bible tells us Jesus knows each of us personally—by name, by heart. He also invites us to do the same—to know Him—by name, by heart. And so He tells us His backstory. Where He grew up. Who influenced Him. What factors shaped His life's path. What's important to Him. What He loves.

On the way, we'll meet the man and woman God chose to be His parents. We'll get to know His aunt and uncle and cousin and hear some of His family's stories from that crazy first year they always seemed to be on the road. Every holy and human moment of Jesus' backstory will give us a little more to know and love about Him. Every road we'll travel leads us to one place—back to Him.

And as we begin to see the bigger picture of Jesus's life and mission, we'll see it's only the beginning of the best story we've ever heard.

Tomorrow: *One on one with an angel with a message*

 Let's talk about it:

True or False? *Everyone you meet has a fascinating backstory.*

1. Ask each other one of these questions about your backstories: *Where did you grow up? Who influenced you most? What factors have shaped your path? What's important to you? What do you love?* For the sake of time, you may have to

limit your response, but use this new understanding of each other to spur more discussion in days to come.

2. Who in Jesus' backstory would you like to know more about?

3. When you think about your spiritual backstory, how do you see God shaping your relationship with Him? Who/what has He used to grow you up in Him?

4. Consider how Philippians 1:6 and Colossians 1:10-14 have been evidenced in your life.

DAY 2

Gabriel

The angel with a message

In the sixth month the angel Gabriel was sent from God to a city of Galilee named Nazareth, to a virgin betrothed to a man whose name was Joseph, of the house of David. And the virgin's name was Mary. And he came to her and said, "Greetings, O favored one, the Lord is with you!"
Luke 1:26-28

As real as this world feels to us, we need only engage our imaginations a little bit to realize another world exists we cannot see or touch. Something in us tells us *that* world is the real world.

That is the angel Gabriel's world. A created reality of power and principalities beyond our dimension. Of heaven's hallways and throne rooms. Of mission and mystery. Of a grandness surpassing space and time, older than the earth.

Our journey through Advent begins in this reality. On that ultimate day, just imagine how the room buzzed with the news. God says it's finally time.

The mission, rustling as a rumor since the first days of creation, is that God Himself will step onto earth—actually *go* there and *become* one of them.

Why would He do that?

"To get His own back," someone supposed.

That was the message Gabriel was to explain to the small, favored ones. He was to unzip the curtain separating our worlds, step through it, and announce the mystery to a young girl and an old man.

"I stand in the presence of God, and I was sent to tell you this good news." The young girl would believe him; the old man, not so much.

To be fair, even Gabriel had a hard time grasping news so good. God of God, Light of Light, very God of very God come down from heaven. *Here*? To do *that*? He and his colleagues would give anything, *anything* to have this gift for themselves. What is beginning here is so strange and wonderful that the host of them dared to peek around the curtain to watch it unfold.

Gabriel's other job was to announce God's human name—*Jesus*. Like a gift, he presented it to the young woman who seemed much too small to carry such a weight. Could she grasp how the universe spun on this Name? Or imagine how someday every knee will bow and every tongue will confess His true sovereignty?

For now, she just whispered it after Gabriel as he said it aloud for the first time.

Tomorrow: *One on one with the man who doubted an angel*

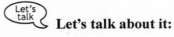 **Let's talk about it:**

Angels are downright fascinating. What do you think about the fact that a whole other world is happening around us that we can't see?

1. How does it make you feel to know that angels are operating in a world around you even though you can't see them?
2. From what you know of the supernatural world, what do you know of the goals of angels and demons?
3. Consider: Ephesians 6:10-20, Hebrews 2, Daniel 9:20-23, Galatians 4:4

DAY 3

Zechariah
The man who doubted an angel

And there appeared to him an angel of the Lord standing on the right side of the altar of incense. And Zechariah was troubled when he saw him, and fear fell upon him. But the angel said to him, "Do not be afraid, Zechariah, for your prayer has been heard, and your wife Elizabeth will bear you a son, and you shall call his name John. And you will have joy and gladness, and many will rejoice at his birth, for he will be great before the Lord. Luke 1:11-15

It's easy to be hard on Zechariah. His disconnect wasn't that an angel showed up with him in the Holy Place. For sure that paralyzed him, but it didn't convince him. Neither did Zechariah doubt who this Gabriel said he was or that an angel knew his name or what he had been praying about for years.

Where Zechariah drew the line was believing his old body could produce a baby. The first time God breaks His 400 years of silence, and He talks to an old man with virility issues.

7

God did a kind thing to help Zechariah believe. Since he had long given up hope for a child, perhaps also hope of a Messiah, God gave him a sign. "You won't be able to speak *until* the day when these things take place."

Not a sound more. Zechariah asked God to prove it and God met his demand. And all through those quiet months, He met Zechariah in the silence and strengthened his faith for this new task of raising a son.

And not just any son, but one who would *go on before the Lord, in the spirit and power of Elijah . . . to prepare a people for the Lord.* His son would play best man to the Messiah. This double blessing flooded the empty place in Zechariah' spirit where his long unanswered prayer had carved a canyon.

So, the time came for his Elizabeth to deliver their son and everyone in the family wanted to name the boy after him, Zechariah. Scribbling on his tablet, he wrote, "His name is John" (as Gabriel had said), and that one word of faith broke Zechariah' silence. With a voice crackling with joy, he burst into worship—not just praise for the new baby boy in the family, but for God remembering the whole family, the family of God.

You have to wonder if Gabriel was in the room for the celebration, a silent witness to the great plan now set in motion. Was he smiling at these "grandparents" cuddling their newborn? Or was he happier for us, for the hope it gives everyone who, like Zechariah, thinks God has forgotten them? That our prayers go unheard. That God is limited to our plans.

Gabriel whispers to us now what's been true for ages: God does the impossible every day.

Tomorrow: *One on one with the girl who said "yes" to God*

Let's talk about it:

On the biggest day of his life and career Zechariah was surprised by an angel who told him something he didn't believe and consequences followed.

1. Can you identify? Have you found it difficult to believe any of God's promises? Which one? How do you counter it with truth?
2. Up until this day, God had not communicated with His people for 400 years. How do you think this influenced Zechariah's response?
3. How was Zechariah's "consequence" God's mercy for him?

══ DAY 4 ══

Mary

The girl who said 'yes' to God

God sent the angel Gabriel to Nazareth, a town in Galilee, to a virgin pledged to be married to a man named Joseph, a descendant of David. The virgin's name was Mary. The angel went to her and said, "Greetings, you who are highly favored! The Lord is with you."
Luke 1:26-28

Most of our lives are lived out on ordinary days.

When she got up that morning, Mary's to-do list was filled with Tuesday sorts of things. Fetch the water. Sweep the courtyard. Feed the animals. If she let herself daydream, there was always Joseph. There would be a beautiful kind of ordinary for them in the never-fancy Nazareth of the first century.

But God had other plans, in place since Eden. History itself turns like a hinge on today's events. Back in heaven, God nodded to Gabriel. It was time.

It's hard to know if Mary was more surprised by Gabriel's sudden appearance, or by his message.

God is with you, Mary. Don't be afraid; He is honoring you.

You will conceive and give birth to a son—He will be called the Son of the Most High.

Wait . . . she recognized that phrase. Son of the Most High . . . *Messiah.* Her people hung every last hope on the promise of Messiah's coming. Every Passover they read Isaiah's prophecy and lifted a glass to His arrival . . . *perhaps this year.*

Gabriel said, "you will bear God's Son—the Messiah."

It was a lot to take in, so Mary started with the practical. *How?*—a question of logistics not faith. Perhaps with a twinkle in his eye, Gabriel answered, *"Nothing is impossible with God."* And he should know, since his job was to stand in God's presence.

Mary's second response confirmed why God picked her in the first place. Instead of probing for details or demanding answers, Mary simply said, "I am the Lord's bond slave. May it be as you have said."

The word is *doulos*—bond slave. In that day, a bond slave gave up freedom to stay with their master. saying instead, "I will freely serve him the rest of my life."

When Jesus came to earth, Philippians 2 tells us He became a *doulos*—a willing servant to His Father's will. Every disciple who has followed since has said the same. *"May it be as you have said"*—loosely translated, "Whatever, Lord." The cost would be high for Mary, but He was her master. She would do what pleases Him.

Later, all by herself again on that ordinary Tuesday, Mary remembered Isaiah's prophecy, *"Therefore the Lord himself will give you a sign. A virgin will conceive and give birth to a son and will call him Immanuel. God with us."*

And she trembled all over, realizing Isaiah was talking about *her.*

Tomorrow: *One on one with the first person to worship Jesus*

11

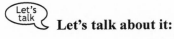 **Let's talk about it:**

Mary's ordinary day turned out to be the turning point of her whole life. (Luke 1:28-38)

1. Think about it—Mary had to set aside her own plans in order to follow God's plans. How was her response a statement of faith?
2. Without fully grasping all that it would mean for her, Mary was willing to be taken beyond her limitations. Martin Luther said, "There were three miracles of the Nativity: that God became man, that a virgin conceived, and that Mary believed. And the greatest of these was the last." What do you think of that?
3. Mary said, "may it be…as you've said." Loosely translated, "whatever You want, Lord." What obstacles to this kind of surrender do you see in this passage? Have you faced this kind of surrender in your life? What did you learn about trusting God?

DAY 5

Elizabeth
The first to worship Jesus

In the days of Herod, king of Judea, there was a priest named Zechariah, of the division of Abijah. And he had a wife from the daughters of Aaron, and her name was Elizabeth. And they were both righteous before God, walking blamelessly in all the commandments and statutes of the Lord. But they had no child, because Elizabeth was barren, and both were advanced in years. Luke 1:5-7

There was a time when she pleaded with God for a child every waking moment of the day, and always through the night. But the heavens were silent and the neighbors were not.

Still, Elizabeth and her husband walked with God. Loyal and loving, they served Him their whole lives—which is why they couldn't explain His confusing, 'No,' when they asked for a child. Around the time their hair got grey, they likely stopped asking. Prayers wear out just like we do.

And now the stage was set. When Zechariah came home speechless from temple the day Gabriel visited him in the Holy Place, he scratched out the cryptic message— "we're going to have a baby."

How Zechariah knew before she did was the first mystery. The second was that he was right. Apparently, God hears old prayers.

Yes, she was pregnant. Her cycles long past, she had no physical sign. She had to wait on God again just like she had in those decades of infertility. Only now, she had a promise from God to cling to.

For the first 20 weeks of this mystery, she stayed close to home. With Zechariah likely deaf as well as mute, the only one to hear her heart was the Lord. And unlike her doubting husband, Elizabeth believed what Gabriel said.

Then after five months—she felt the first flutter of a child. *Alive.* It's true! Her public disgrace finally over, she told the neighbors how God had upended the natural order. *This is the Lord's doing.*

The next month when her young niece from Galilee unexpectedly showed up at her door and called out *hello,* Elizabeth's baby danced a jig in her womb. In that moment, Elizabeth absolutely *knew* Gabriel was right. He told Zechariah their son would prepare the way for Messiah. Now the Messiah, in that young virgin's womb, waited on her doorstep. Hugging her niece, she embraced the Child in Mary's womb—the miracle Messiah come to save us. The young and the old laughed until they cried with God's miracle in their bellies. If the neighbors were watching then, they knew for sure something was up.

And all those years Elizabeth prayed for a child? When finally, she nuzzled newborn John in her arms, she couldn't remember the sorrow at all. If she had known then what she knew now, the waiting would have passed in a flash.

Tomorrow: *One on one with the teenager who knew God's Word*

Let's talk about it:

Elizabeth had waited a long time for God to give her and her husband a baby. Imagine how surprised she was to finally learn of her role in this miracle.

1. Elizabeth was probably in her 50s when she was told she was going to have a baby. Why do you think she made a really good mom for John the Baptist?
2. Discuss your thoughts of the line, "Apparently, God hears old prayers."
3. What's the longest you've prayed for something? How does Elizabeth's example encourage/challenge you?

DAY 6

Mary Sang
The teen who knew God's Word

And Mary said, "My soul magnifies the Lord, and my spirit rejoices in God my Savior, for he has looked on the humble estate of his servant. For behold, from now on all generations will call me blessed; for he who is mighty has done great things for me, and holy is his name. Luke 1:46-49

For five days she walked. *Thinking. Praying.* South to Jerusalem. To her aunt, Elizabeth. Processing, *What just happened?*

Mary grew up believing God was present with His people, even in His silence. She knew God promised Abraham a great nation. God handpicked Moses to get her people out of Egypt. God parted the Red Sea and fed her people for forty years in the desert. God gave them this land. God was behind everything; she just knew it.

She knew God promised them a Messiah. Every Passover she set an extra cup at the table for Elijah in case he stopped in to say the Messiah is here at last. Her family left the door open for him.

So, when Gabriel told her the Messiah was on His way, it didn't catch them off-guard. The surprise was, at this minute He was moving inside her womb.

On her 90-mile walk south, when only she and Gabriel knew this unfolding plan, Mary likely called from memory every Scripture she ever heard about the Messiah. Who He was. What He would do. What did the prophet Isaiah say? What were Daniel's prophecies? The Psalms? The Bible had been the soundtrack of her home, and now she sang it softly to herself.

At this critical turning point, she trusted the God she grew up believing. She released the hundred reasons this should not be and simply said, "Whatever You want, Lord." Her heart beat faster with her choice now made.

All it took to let her secret out was showing up at Elizabeth's door. At Mary's hello, baby John—still in Elizabeth's womb—skipped like a lamb. Without Mary saying a word, Elizabeth guessed her secret. With a hug, "You're blessed among women, my sweet girl, because you believe what God said; you believe every word."

In all the confusing mix of breathtaking privilege and unspeakable pain Mary had pondered in those 90 miles, her faith and joy came bubbling out in worship to God.

"Yes, can you believe it?" she burst into a praise song which wove together twelve Old Testament promises answered in Messiah's coming. She entered the mystery with confidence.

Mary had believed God's Word her whole life, and now she stepped *into* the most significant story of all.

Tomorrow: *One on one with the man who believed the impossible*

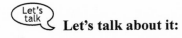 **Let's talk about it:**

Mary knew God's Word (the Old Testament). She likely had memorized large portions.

1. Mary's song and prayer (Luke 1:46-55) gives evidence that she knew the promises of God very well and even had a lot of scripture memorized.
2. Do you know any Scripture by heart? What would you like to memorize and remember during life's important moments?

DAY 7

Joseph
The man who believed the impossible

When Joseph woke from sleep, he did as the angel of the Lord commanded him: he took his wife, but knew her not until she had given birth to a son. And he called his name Jesus. Matthew 1:24-25

When Joseph heard Mary's shocking news, his trust in her shattered.

The woman he loves, the one he pledged his commitment to before God and kept pure despite his own desires—disappears for three months and comes home pregnant? *What was he supposed to think?*

Mary said she hadn't betrayed him, but how could he believe her?

What he needed now was a plan. A righteous man, Joseph would do the right thing, even if it cost him. By law he could break their betrothal. He could have Mary stoned to death for adultery, if he wanted. But Joseph loved her. He didn't want revenge, just a way out of this mess. Why make it worse for her now that she was destined for a life of shame and poverty? He decided to put her away privately to raise the child alone.

That's the only plan Joseph could live with, the only one that allowed him to sleep.

But God has another solution. An angel, likely Gabriel, visits Joseph in a dream and whispers to the devastated man, *"Don't be afraid to take Mary as your wife; for the Child who has been conceived in her is of the Holy Spirit."*

And then the story changed. Joseph wakes up, puts his frantic plans to rest, and however incomplete the picture, decides to believe God.

But what if he hadn't? He could have walked away. Nursed Mary's "betrayal." Defended his manhood rather than protect her. What if Joseph thought it too big a risk to believe a dream?

Then God would have had provided another man to be Mary's strength in the wonder and wounding of this mystery. Someone else would have stood by her in labor. Someone else would have loved and provided for Jesus. Someone else would have taught Jesus the Law and the prophets, a trade craft, and what it means to be a man. Jesus would have called another man, *Abba*.

The trajectory of another man's life would have changed that night when God asked the impossible—to believe this fragile news and play a part in this His story.

God's purposes will not be stopped. Trust Him with crazy obedience or miss the opportunity.

Some moments in your life set the course of who you're going to be. Usually subtle, you never see them coming. Suddenly one moment of faith changes everything. *Am I willing to imagine another kind of life? Could God's dream be bigger?*

No doubt Joseph and Mary's lives were harder than they expected. No one will ever know what it cost them. But to have the privilege of loving Jesus in this unique way? They wouldn't have traded that, no, not for the world.

Tomorrow: *One on one with the voice crying in the desert*

Let's talk about it:

Sometimes life doesn't go as planned. Just ask Joseph.

1. Why might some call Joseph, "the hero behind the scenes." What was Joseph's greatest step of faith?
2. What character traits do you see evident in Joseph's response to the angel's direction to take Mary as his wife?
3. Discuss the line, "God's purposes will not be stopped. Trust Him with crazy obedience or miss the opportunity."

DAY 8

John
The voice that cried in the wilderness

Now the time came for Elizabeth to give birth, and she bore a son. And her neighbors and relatives heard that the Lord had shown great mercy to her, and they rejoiced with her. And on the eighth day they came to circumcise the child. And they would have called him Zechariah after his father, but his mother answered, "No; he shall be called John."
Luke 1:57-60

Like doting parents will do, Zechariah and Elizabeth reminded John every day how their old prayers brought him to them and why. John knew before he could tie his own sandals that his life was wrapped around a mission.

From the womb, Elizabeth knew her boy was linked to something supernatural. And you can be sure when Zechariah taught John the Law and prophets, they paid special attention to every mention of the Messiah. Zechariah echoed the prophets who said the forerunner to the Messiah would "guide our feet into the way of peace." *And look,* in his dad's imagination, *there's John's footprints, forging a path out of the Old Testament into a new and living way.*

That was their boy. Precocious, spirited, the apple of his father's eye, the joy of his mother's heart. And it's not a leap to think his Aunt Mary had a special affection for him. But no relationship would have been more layered and profound than John's connection with his cousin, Jesus.

When they were boys of a certain age and the family visited from the Galilee on feast days, likely John and Jesus wandered the hills around Jerusalem with a dog in tow and plenty of sticks. Even then John could charm the bees out of their honey.

Perhaps, the bond between them—tighter than kinship—tied them to a future they both saw somehow. John may not have known then what he would know later about his younger cousin, but the Spirit in him whispered that everything revolved around Jesus.

The lesser and the greater, who one day would call the lesser the greatest among men (Luke 7:28).

As John grew, a roughness settled in him. He looked wild, bound by the Levite rule not to cut his hair. But neither could his spirit be constrained by the rules of culture.

Everyone knew John belonged somewhere outside, in the wilderness where God always calls His people. Where he could say what needed to be said.

John left his father's house, his father's town and profession. Jerusalem had never been home for him, anyway. He would be a new Elijah—with a character, shaped by courage, who shot out of their family history like a shooting star. Bright. Hot. Short-lived.

When people asked, "Why hasn't God spoken to us all these 400 years?" the next voice they heard was John's, coming from the general direction of the Judean wilderness.

Clear and to the point, his voice carried on the wind, "Get ready."

Tomorrow: *One on one with the amazing women in Jesus' backstory*

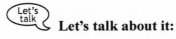

Let's talk about it:

Is John the Baptist an Old Testament or New Testament saint? Some would say he's both.

1. From what John preached and how he lived, what message did he want people to understand? What do you think attracted people to John?
2. Why is "repentance" such a big deal? Consider Bible characters who repented or refused to repent—what lessons can we learn from them?

DAY 9

Jesus' Back Story
The women of Christmas

"And Ram the father of Amminadab, and Amminadab the father of Nahshon, and Nahshon the father of Salmon, and Salmon the father of Boaz by Rahab, and Boaz the father of Obed by Ruth, and Obed the father of Jesse, and Jesse the father of David the king." Matthew 1:4-6

Before you get to the manger, a long list of names interrupts the Christmas story. Look closely at that list of "begats;" in the first chapter of Matthew and four names will pop out as unusual. Gentile names—which normally don't belong in a proper record of Jewish heritage. Certainly not in a kingly line.

But there they are. Gentiles. And women, no less.

The first, **Rahab.** She lived in Jericho at the time when the children of Israel were ending their long walk from Egypt when rumors of invasion worried those who lived on the city walls. Perhaps if we heard more of her story, we'd understand how Rahab ended up in this desperate life (she's known as "the harlot"). All we know is the spies Joshua sent climbed in her window and she protected them instead of herself. As it happens, they ended up saving her and her family. Later when asked by her grandchildren why she let that red rope out her window as a signal, she said she had heard about the Messiah and just knew this was the way she could get pulled in. (Read Rahab's story in Joshua 6:15-25.)

The next name in Matthew's genealogy, surprisingly, is Rahab's daughter-in-law, **Ruth.** Though their stories are rarely linked, Ruth married Rahab's son, Boaz. Ruth from Moab—which is like saying Ruth, from the wrong side of town. No one dared say that to this faithful girl who survived her own share of grief and came out all the sweeter. She left her own home to take her mother-in-law, Naomi, back to Bethlehem. Two widows, one old and bitter, one tender and young walked into town and heads turned. Especially attentive was the eligible bachelor, Boaz. And the romancing of the most divine kind commenced. Years later, Naomi's joy was restored when she bounced her grandson on her knee, the boy who would be the grandfather to King David himself. (Read Ruth's story in the short book of Ruth.)

But that almost didn't happen. Back in Genesis when all the attention was on Joseph and his colorful coat, Jacob's oldest son, Judah, got weary of the family drama. So much so he almost broke the line from Adam to David by refusing his daughter-in-law, **Tamar,** twice a widow by his two sons, the right to have a child by his third son. Rather than risk it ("she's bad luck!") he pushed her aside. Perhaps Tamar knew, beyond her own needs, what a mistake this was and figured out a plan to keep the family line going. As shady as we think that plan was, it was exactly what Judah needed to wake up. Later, he called Tamar a blessing, worthy of honor, and her grandchildren would name their little girls after her. (Read Tamar's story in Genesis 38.)

And the last woman we read of only as David's wife, but we know it's **Bathsheba.** How much she was victimized or how much she cooperated in David's ugly sin, we don't know. All we know for sure is his story became hers and her life with Uriah got snuffed out. Instead, she ended up in the palace, married to a man overwhelmed by guilt. From Bathsheba, we learn that even when sin separates us, God doesn't give up on His own. When we ask Him, He creates new hearts from shattered pieces. As for David and Bathsheba— the child of their child a thousand years yet future would die to make them whole. That Redeemer of every man's story would be everything David dreamed about and more. (Read Bathsheba's story in 2 Samuel 11.)

The red thread connecting every story? Faith in God. Beyond the grief, the guilt, the poverty of their lives, these women in Jesus' line believed God. Somehow. We're not certain of the details but we know in the end, their wounds healed. And God wanted His grace—and their stories—to go on record.

Tomorrow: *One on one with Jesus' parents on the way to Bethlehem*

 Let's talk about it:

Jesus' backstory is filled with fascinating people.

1. Of these four women, what stands out to you as a universal lesson? What specific lessons can we apply from their situations?
2. Of the four women—Ruth, Rahab, Tamar, and Bathsheba— whose backstory is interesting to you; who would you like to study more?
3. Where are the surprises for you? How does that encourage/ challenge you in your own story?

DAY 10

The Long Walk South

What Joseph and Mary might have thought

In those days a decree went out from Caesar Augustus that all the world should be registered . . .And all went to be registered, each to his own town. And Joseph also went up from Galilee, from the town of Nazareth, to Judea, to the city of David, which is called Bethlehem, because he was of the house and lineage of David, to be registered with Mary, his betrothed, who was with child. Luke 2:1-5

She's amazing. Look at how she keeps up with the caravan, walking just as well as women without babies in their belly. Remember to offer her water more—90 miles is a long way. Five days. Not once has she complained of the heat or the road. But she's never complained of anything, not in these six months we've shared side by side.

He's amazing. He's never left my side. Other husbands abandon their wives to walk with the men. Laughing, daring, shoving, solving the world's problems—the men become boys again. That was my Joseph before our calling. I may carry this child in my belly, but he carries the weight of it all on his shoulders. Now he smiles more than he laughs. Slow smiles with deep eyes.

We've got to keep up. How can I help her? If we're not with the others when we reach the river, we'll be in trouble. I can't protect her there. We can't walk the river path alone. Too many dangers. And we can't bed there. We must stay with the group. El Shaddai, help me know how to help her.

Where will we stay in Bethlehem? Ain Karim is close, perhaps with Zechariah and Elizabeth? She could help when my time comes. We could see baby John. Zechariah could encourage Joseph. No, don't plan, let Joseph provide for you. But he did ask me to confide in him; never again to run without a word. Should I suggest Elizabeth's? Do we have enough to pay the tax? Oy, a kick. Hello, *hamud*, little cutey. Are you almost ready to meet the world?

Her hand in mine feels so good. Her grip firm, so determined. One hand in mine, one on the child. I will help you, Mary, I promise you. God, I promise You.

His hand so strong. I miss Abba. What would he think about this wonderful, frightening thing? That the Mashiach we prayed to come is here under my heart. His grandson. Abba, do you see me from heaven? Do you understand this mystery? The Mighty One has done great things . . . for me.

For me, Abba. For you. Holy is His name. Just as you taught me to pray. His mercy is upon generation after generation toward those who fear Him. You taught me to fear Him, Abba. This blessing is yours, too. Yes, even this pain. *<Breathe, breathe.>*

I hope my cousins got word of when to expect us. That there will be a place for us. I couldn't leave her in Nazareth. These six months have been hard enough. Too many raised eyebrows counting the moons since I brought Mary home. Too many whispers. Yet never an unkind word from Mary. My Mary. When we get back it will be better; the baby will be with us. Everyone loves a baby. But they will wonder why his name is Jesus and not Joseph.

You must help me, El Shaddai. I am not as wise as others You could have chosen to bear Your child. Thank You for this good man. We don't know what to do, but our eyes are on You.

Would she like to ride the ass? "Only when I need to," she had said. My brave Mary. We will save the donkey till the final day—20 miles uphill from Jericho to the heights. Frightening turns and deadly drops. Bandits in the shadows. We must keep up. Help us, Jehovah Sabaoth, Lord of hosts. I am afraid of all that is ahead for us.

"Here, Mary, have some water."

"*Toda, ahava shelli*; Thank you, my love."

Tomorrow: *One on one with the one who cared for Mary*

 Let's talk about it:

The Bible frequently describes the Christian life as "a walk." In a sense, the Lord has invited you for a walk with Him, together on this journey through life.

1. Explore this metaphor in some key New Testament verses:
   - *Colossians 2:6   *Galatians 5:16   *Galatians 5:25
   - * Ephesians 4:1, 5:2, 5:8, 5:15   *Romans 8:1

   What about this metaphor of walking with God appeals to you?

2. When you walk, you focus on the next step. Same is true in the Christian life—it's a series of small steps, small progresses, in one direction. In every walk of faith, you must focus on the next step God has asked you to take. Consider this in the place you stand today. What step of faith do you need to take next? Help each other see what it means to walk by faith in the details of your lives.

DAY 11

Joseph
The husband who did the next thing

 *But you, O Bethlehem Ephrathah, who are too little to be among the clans of Judah, from you shall come forth for me one who is to be ruler in Israel, whose coming forth is from of old, from ancient days.* **Micah 5:2**

Did I miss something?

Joseph got Mary safely to Bethlehem. He found a place to protect her while she rested, a place where she could give birth. In a sense, he did his job. But you have to wonder if the six months of crisis—culminating now in this makeshift birthing stall—made Joseph wonder if he had messed up somehow.

This is not how I would have planned it. This special child would have been born in Nazareth, not Bethlehem. Or Jerusalem even, where our people could help. There should be midwives, not farm animals. An actual bed, not just hay. And at the baby's first cry, friends and family and neighbors should erupt in celebration. Here we just have stars. A sky full of silent stars. We are alone.

As Joseph paced under those stars, was he frustrated? Or frightened? Did he pray? *I've done what You've asked of me, God, but it doesn't feel right. When the angel told me this plan was of Your*

31

making, I think I expected something other than a stable for the birth of Your Son. If it was my son, I would have planned it better . . . Mary has been nothing but faithful to You. Uncomplaining. A quiet spirit. Willing. She expects me to do right by her. To do right by You. So, is this right or did we miss something?

What do you do when you feel caught between all that you know to do and what makes sense? It may not seem like it, but you do have options.

Option A: Reverse course. You can go back to what feels right to you.

Option B: Stand still, move neither forward nor back. Freeze in place out of fear of doing something wrong.

Option C: Do the next thing. You always know one thing you can do and so by faith you do that, trusting God you're moving in the right direction.

And that's what makes Joseph God's man for the job. He did the next thing. When the angel told him to take Mary as his wife, he did it. When Mary explained her encounter with Gabriel, he listened and believed her. When God prompted him to go to Bethlehem (to fulfill Micah 5:2 prophecy), he went. Soon he'll be asked to pack up his young family and hide from Herod in Egypt, and he will obey again.

As important as he was to the story, Joseph only saw a small piece of the big picture. We know more than he ever did. But God gave him enough light on a dark path to take the next step, and he took it.

Most of our questions won't get answered until heaven. But like Joseph, we will always be given enough light to take the next step all the way there.

Tomorrow: *One on one with Jesus, His story from heaven's perspective*

Let's talk about it:

Even though it was one of the greatest nights in history, the night Jesus was born felt quite ordinary to Joseph and Mary.

1. Consider the three options presented here for when you face a seemingly impossible situation. How do you identify with these—or agree/disagree?

2. What is the singular decision in Option C? How does 2 Corinthians 5:7 factor into our choices?

━━ DAY 12 ━━

The Song

Christmas from a heavenly perspective

Have this mind among yourselves, which is yours in Christ Jesus, who, though he was in the form of God, did not count equality with God a thing to be grasped, but emptied himself, by taking the form of a servant, being born in the likeness of men.
Philippians 2:5-7

Great stories always include surprise reversals.

Luke 2 tells the Christmas story from earth's perspective. Philippians 2:5-11 tells the same story from heaven's perspective. The ancients sang it as a song:

"Though Jesus was God, He did not demand and cling to His rights as God

God the Son humbled Himself to become approachable majesty. He set aside His right to all of heaven's joy and said to the Father, "I will go." The One who always existed, put on skin so we could see the God who cannot be seen (Colossians 1:15).

... "He laid aside His mighty power and glory

Fully God in every way, Jesus lived here with us. Like a king who took off his crown and robe, He gave up honor for fellowship.

He ate and laughed at our tables (2 Corinthians 8:9). He poured out every glorious thing He deserved—if only to save just one of us.

. . . "Taking the disguise of a slave and becoming like men

Nobody knew Jesus was God by looking at Him. He cried like any baby. He ran on the hills around Nazareth. He learned a trade. He grieved when Joseph died. He got hungry and sleepy. 100% human and 100% God. How crazy that God could fit into our frame (Luke 22:27).

. . . And He humbled himself even further . . . to die a criminal's death on a cross

Jesus arrived, knowing one day He would pay the ultimate price for those He loved. That's the gift of Christmas. Who Joseph and Mary protected and nurtured in their home would be executed, taking the punishment for what separates us all from life in God.

. . . At the name of Jesus every knee should bow, in heaven and on earth and under the earth, and every tongue confess that Jesus Christ is Lord . . .

But once He finished the job He came to do, God raised Jesus from the dead. His blood satisfied the payment for sin, and now we can be saved. And the glory, honor, and privilege Jesus set aside? God gave it all back to Him. (Hebrews 1:3).

One day soon, the reversal will be complete when every person from history will say, "Jesus Christ is Lord." Say it now, and you'll have the life in God that Jesus died to make possible, and you will be saved from deserved judgement. Sing it now in worship to Jesus, your Savior.

Father, You said that "if I confess Jesus as Lord with my mouth, and believe in my heart God raised Him from the dead, I will be saved." I believe what You've said about Jesus dying in my place to pay for my sin. Please save me. I confess Jesus as my Lord and Savior today and will gladly do it forever in heaven. Amen.

Tomorrow: *One on one with the ones who fell out of heaven*

Let's talk about it:

The Old Testament is clear Jesus existed and interacted with people before He came as a baby.

1. Explore Colossians 1:15-20 and discuss Jesus as Creator and Sustainer of the universe. What are your favorite parts of this passage?
2. Read Philippians 2:5-8 together. This passage gives us a snapshot of Jesus' decision to come to earth as a baby, in obedience to His Fathers instructions. This passage highlights Jesus' humility. How would you define humility? What did it look like in Jesus' life? What does it look like in the lives of people you admire? Consider for yourself what humility looks like in your life.

DAY 13

Angels
The Ones who cheered

And suddenly there was with the angel a multitude of the heavenly host praising God and saying, "Glory to God in the highest, and on earth peace among those with whom he is pleased!". Luke 2:14-15

It was like they just had to tell us on earth what everyone knew in heaven: *An amazing thing just happened!*

So perhaps the largest group the angels could find in Bethlehem were Bedouins huddled on a rocky slope outside of town tending sheep. One angel opened a window to the heavenlies and turned up the volume.

"Hey—did you hear? He's here, you lucky people! Today is the day! God kept His word."

And just like that, angels flooded the night sky like fireflies. Contrary to the stories, they didn't sing—no, they shouted! They cheered like they were at a football game—back and forth to each other like fans gone wild. Literally, Scripture said "they let loose."

"He's come! He's here! He's the gift that saves lives. Glory to God in the highest!"

Ever since Eden, they had been watching for God's promised plan to ransom creation from evil. Lately, rumors in the halls of heaven said a heavenly invasion was imminent, a plan hell-bent on destroying evil in the world. When the angels heard the formal announcement, all heaven broke loose.

Over in the stable, the sweet newborn tucked in a makeshift crib, slept through it all. But to the angels, there was God Himself, swaddled in flesh. Mystery in a manger. On a mission to wage war. Come to rescue a hijacked creation. A baby's cry signaled the beginning of a revolution. And the metanarrative of history spiraling downward since Eden took a sharp turn upward.

Sometimes wonder is in the mystery; other times wonder is in the understanding. The angels understood what was happening, at least a little.

"Unto you is born this day, your Savior." Here to rescue you like you were the only one in the world needing saving. One for one.

Joy to the world—your Savior has come. Explore that wonder in your head. Let it comfort your heart. Bow to His majesty.

Tomorrow: *One on one with one of the shepherds*

 Let's talk about it:

Picture the shepherds, going about their task as usual, when the night sky split open and countless bright shining beings filled the darkness.

1. Consider the scene from a heavenly perspective. What did the angels know about Jesus? Read aloud: Isaiah 9:6, Luke 2:8-14.
2. Consider the line, "Sometimes wonder is in the mystery; other times wonder is in the understanding." How do you see this as true—for the angels? For the shepherds? For us?

DAY 14

Shepherds, Part 1

The ones who were told first

 *When the angels went away from them into heaven, the shepherds said to one another, "Let us go over to Bethlehem and see this thing that has happened, which the Lord has made known to us." And they went with haste and found Mary and Joseph, and the baby lying in a manger. And when they saw it, they made known the saying that had been told them concerning this child. And all who heard it wondered at what the shepherds told them. Luke 2:15-18*

You've heard us tell our story; I doubt I could add anything new. I deny none of it. If we didn't all see the same thing, I would have thought we drank bad wine. Midnight visions.

The night we saw the spirits in the sky marked my life. He found me there in the darkness an angry, confused, young man. I say He found me, when really, we found Him just as the spirit said we would, a baby in a trough. A poor couple who looked as hopeless as we did. She was my age. Her firstborn, by the looks of her.

I was barely thirteen, with little in my future except to do what my father and uncles did—tend sheep. I hate sheep. And this flock on Migdal Eder were sold on Temple Mount for sacrifice. They had about as much hope as I did, a Jew pinned under a Roman boot.

Ama said she worried for me with this anger inside. Abba, may he rest in peace, said I would work it out as young men do. She feared I would become a zealot, what with the unrest flaring up around our troubled land.

What were we to think when the spirits announced, "Good news"? Caesar's birthday was called "The Good News." Caesar wanted us to worship him as "Savior of the world"—and call his heir, "the Son of God." We had to bow to Caesar and call him, "King of Kings and Lord of Lords" and if you didn't bow, they impaled you on a stake until you died.

Do you see why the spirit's message confused me? They filled the night sky with such light—and then they were gone, like smoke into the heavens.

Are we still alive? I first thought. *What just happened?* Then I heard my father singing and laughing, "Get up brothers; on your feet! Let's go, son! Didn't you hear what he said? We're going to Bethlehem!"

My father, may he rest in peace, never got over that night. He talked about it to everyone who bought a lamb from him in the temple. He told the sheep when no one else was around. "I saw the Messiah," he would say. "We followed the spirit's direction until we found them in the cave —the three of them nestled together in lantern light. Such a place for the Messiah to be born!" he marveled. "Had the spirits not told us, we would have missed it. We who are not allowed to worship in the temple got to see glory in the field! Can you believe it? Messengers from the Almighty (bless His holy name) kibitzing in the field with shepherds! Good tidings of great joy which shall be to all people! Yes, all people—but do you know who they told first? Us!" And he would throw back his head and laugh, "They told us!"

Yes, my father died a happy man.

But I lived a haunted life. Disturbed by questions never answered. Was that baby the Messiah? How could He have been the Savior—He looked like any other baby. In all the years since, I've been troubled by the beauty of that night in such a dark time. He found me, alright. And I've been looking for Him everywhere since. (...to be continued in Part Two.)

Tomorrow: *One on one with what could have happened*

 Let's talk about it:

Unless you happen to be in the Bethlehem field that night and saw the angels announcing Jesus' birth, you would never have realized something big happened

1. Why do you think God chose to announce Jesus' birth to shepherds (a very small, disrespected pocket society?)
2. What people think is important and what God thinks is important is sometimes flipped upside down. What is something that people put a high priority on but God doesn't? What does God value, yet people don't? How does this perspective influence your priorities?

Can you recall times when God showed up in your life and unexpected way or through an unexpected person?

DAY 15

He Could Have Just
The Savior who chose us

"For the Son of Man came to seek and to save the lost." Luke 19:10

He could have just "appeared" as King and skipped the manger scene.

He could have seen to it Mary had a clean room for His birth.
He could have chosen a wealthier, more comfortable family.
He could have settled down in Galilee, married a nice girl, and raised good kids.

He could have turned stones into bread in the desert.
He could have silenced Satan and his tempting offers once and for all.
He could have created a new heaven and earth right then and skipped running around Galilee.

He could have left the world in darkness, aborted the rescue plan, left us to wander on our own.

He could have commanded obedience from everyone He met as easily as He ordered the wind and waves to be quiet.

He could have demanded a thousand angels rescue Him in Gethsemane.

He could have brought Herod, and Pilate, and Caesar Augustus to their knees, then and there.

He could have come down from the cross and saved Himself.

He could have come when crucifixions were out of style.

He could have gone right to heaven from the grave and left us all to wonder if He was who He said He was.

He could have done it all a lot quicker, a lot grander—without the humiliation, without the humanity.

But He didn't.

Because He was Emmanuel—God with us.

Because although people needed a Messiah to redeem them, a King to rule them, they first needed a Shepherd to walk with them, seeking lost sheep along our roads. A tender Savior who didn't mind the smelly straw and silly questions and would love the people who struggled with sin and doubt and strong wills. A Savior who wouldn't trade the lives of those He cherished for Calvary's atrocities.

The question has never been what Jesus Christ could have done but instead, what He chose to do.

For us.

Tomorrow: *One on one with Jesus' mom*

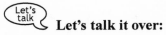 **Let's talk it over:**

God does things differently than we would. This devotional lists a couple scenarios that would make more sense to us.

1. Which scenarios make the most sense to you?
2. What does "Emmanuel—God with us" mean to you?

DAY 16

20 Questions for Mary:
What would you ask her?

"And his father and his mother marveled at what was said about him". Luke 2:33

1. Did you ever wonder, *why me? How was I chosen by God to be the Messiah's mom?*

2. Were you surprised the first time you felt the flutter of life in your tummy?

3. How did your family react when you told them about Gabriel's visit and what he said?

4. Did you cry when Elizabeth greeted you so warmly? S*he knew!* Did you compare your cravings, your morning sickness, your ankles swelling?

5. Was telling Joseph your news the hardest thing you've ever done? Did you think you might have to raise this baby alone?

6. How did you deal with the shameful looks and criticism from the ladies in Nazareth? Did Joseph comfort you? Did he help you refocus on the truth?

7. Did you *have to* go with Joseph to Bethlehem or did you just not want to be without him in Nazareth? Did you know about the prophecy that Messiah was to be born in Bethlehem?

8. Was anyone with you when the labor pains intensified and the baby was coming? Were you frightened? Did Joseph break with tradition and help you?

9. Did you count newborn Jesus' fingers and toes? Who did He look like? Did He have your nose or your eyes?

10. Did you mind the clumsy intrusion of the shepherds into your private space? What did you think of their story about the angels in the field?

11. How was Joseph with the baby? Did he mind naming him Jesus, rather than Joe, Jr.? Did he pick Jesus up when He cried? Change His diaper? Did you ever eavesdrop on him talking to Him? What did he say?

12. When did Jesus first sleep through the night? What songs did you sing to Him during 3 a.m. feedings? Did you hum Him the Psalms?

13. What's with the old man in the temple? Did you wonder how he knew your boy was the Messiah? And his odd prediction of the sword? And what about the travelers from the East? How could they have known your secret? Did you realize then that their gifts were God's provision for your family?

14. Did you believe Joseph when he told you about his dream of angels and warnings of Herod's plot? What was it like to know someone wanted to kill your baby? Did you pray for the mothers whose babies were murdered in the search for yours?

15. What was it like to raise a kid who didn't sin? Did you feel guilty every time you did?

16. What were Jesus' first words? His favorite foods? Did He have a pet? Did He play well with His half-brothers and sisters? With cousin John?

17. Did you ever keep his fingers away from Joseph's spikes and hammers —not imagining the cruel scene someday.

18. Did you ever cry to God for help in knowing how to be His mom? Did you ever feel like God should have chosen someone else? Someone older, wiser? Someone who could have given Jesus a better life?

19. Did you ever look at this sweet little boy, God's little boy, and think of the amazing truth that He was the Christ, the Messiah, the Savior of the world . . . and that He was your Savior?

20. How did you feel when it was time for Him to leave your home? Or that day on the Mount of Olives when He disappeared in the clouds?

Tomorrow: *One on one with the old man who held God*

 Let's talk about it:

Mary, an ordinary girl God used in an extraordinary situation, has a story to tell.

1. Which of these questions made you pause and wonder about her answer?
2. What other question would you like to ask her?

47

DAY 17

Simeon
The man who waited for the promise

Now there was a man in Jerusalem, whose name was Simeon, and this man was righteous and devout, waiting for the consolation of Israel, and the Holy Spirit was upon him. And it had been revealed to him by the Holy Spirit that he would not see death before he had seen the Lord's Christ. Luke 2:25-26

Time was running out for Simeon. God promised the old man he wouldn't die till he saw the Messiah. To Simeon, this was a dream. Day after month after year he showed up in the temple, praying for Israel, studying each young man's face—*Are you Mashiach?* He was sure he would recognize Him when he saw Him.

Hope like that keeps you alive.

Imagine the moment, then, when Simeon looked up from his temple post and saw the young couple crossing the courtyard. One cradled a baby, the other carried a basket with two pigeons, a poor man's substitute for a sacrificial lamb.

The Spirit of God whispered to Simeon, *There He is!*
What? Our Deliverer is a baby?

The couple no doubt felt strange to have their secret out in this holy place; they knew their boy was special . . . from God . . . but now a perfect stranger wept as he held out his arms. *May I hold Him?*

And Jesus, wide-eyed for His six weeks in the world, thrashed His limbs with excitement. Mary and Joseph's eyes met, still shy to the attention.

"He's here." Simeon cried, "The Lord's salvation is here!" And he looked with faith into the eyes of God Himself.

Then Simeon's expression changed. The noise of the courtyard—bleating lambs, rushing crowds, merchants, sinners, and priests—narrowed to silence. A shadow moved across his face.

What Simeon saw was a long way off, but its grief was as real as this gift in his arms. The Messiah's arrival also meant suffering to come: a mother's heart pierced, a nation divided, a perfect man's horrific sacrifice. Simeon's patient faith gave him God's eyes. And this view through a glass darkly was sorrow and joy mixed and as long as eternity.

Perhaps later that day or week, Simeon rode out of this life a satisfied man, full of everything God had promised him.

Rest in peace, Simeon.

Tomorrow: *One on one with the woman who prayed for Jesus all her life*

Let's talk about it:

We're not told how long Simeon waited for God to fill His promise but we can guess it was a long time.

1. What's the longest you've waited for something?
2. Simeon's story resonates with a lot of people. Why do you think that is?
3. What temptations do we face when we wait on God? What good work does God do in us while we wait for Him? Consider: Romans 5:3-5, Isaiah 30:18, Psalm 37:3-7

══ DAY 18 ══

Anna
The woman who prayed

And there was a prophetess, Anna, the daughter of Phanuel, of the tribe of Asher. She was advanced in years, having lived with her husband seven years from when she was a virgin, and then as a widow until she was eighty-four. She did not depart from the temple, worshiping with fasting and prayer night and day.
Luke 2:36-37

Her name means "gracious" and as a pleasant coincidence, it happened to be true. Anna was old *and* wise. Old, you can't help. Wise is another matter. The deep ones have seen their share of tragedy and lived to tell how in the end, God does all things well.

Ask anyone who has walked with God for more than 30 years and they'll tell you that godliness is a process, a series of choices. Nothing takes the place of long conversations with God. That's what Anna had done in the temple, year after year.

A young woman in 63 B.C., Anna witnessed Rome take over Jerusalem. Perhaps that's when her husband died. In her time, she watched Herod's great temple building project begin and nearly finish. The incessant political crisis would have been enough for her to fast and pray in the temple, pleading with God for the long-promised Messiah who she envisioned to be Israel's political savior.

So, Anna planted herself in the temple, the hub of Jewish faith at the center of the busiest spot in the city. As a widow, she relied on the faith community for her life. In return, she held babies, laughed with mothers, and prayed for families. She nurtured no bitterness for what she lacked, only praise for how much she had and prayers for what she hoped would come.

And it did come. When she saw Simeon, tears streaming down his cheeks lift the newborn baby in the temple's filtered sunlight, she knew right away the Messiah was here.

Imagine her holding out her arms to cuddle Jesus that day!

What else could she say than "thanks be to God"? Though she had plenty to add later—telling everyone she met about this baby and the hope He brought to the entire world. Anna's arms held the Messiah.

She had traded youth for a miracle.

Tomorrow: *One on one with a madman*

 Let's talk about it:

In the first century, Anna was about as desperate as they come. She was elderly, a widow and completely dependent on others for survival.

1. What lessons in attitude can we learn from Anna?
2. Consider the lessons you've learned from older generations. How does walking with God for a lifetime influence your perspective in times of crisis? Is wisdom guaranteed?

DAY 19

Herod
A Study in Madness

When Herod the king heard this, he was troubled, and all Jerusalem with him; and assembling all the chief priests and scribes of the people, he inquired of them where the Christ was to be born. Matthew 2:1-4

In every generation, madmen walk the earth, scattering terror like seeds. The year Jesus was born, his name was Herod. Let's call him, Herod, the wish-I-was-great.

His 33-year reign over Israel reads like a clinical study in paranoia. Assassinating at whim, his name sent shivers up the spine of a nation.

Herod hungered for Jewish respect and tried to bribe them for it. He built them a temple complex that rivaled any wonder of the world. He crafted coliseums, aqueducts, and palaces that continue to marvel Holy Land pilgrims today. But Israel despised Herod for his half-breed lineage, his unbridled ambition, and the river of blood cascading off his throne like a waterfall.

Herod's shock and awe strategies that failed to win the Jewish people's hearts, won him Rome's attention. Early in his career, he played a role in the soap opera starring Cleopatra, Marc Antony, and Julius Caesar which unfolded just over the border in Egypt. Rome rewarded Herod's cutthroat service with the throne of Israel, a country he had no right to rule.

With the cruelties that served him in war and intrigue, Herod dominated Israel with a bloody fist. Living in the palace was especially dangerous. Herod slaughtered hundreds of "disloyal" family and workers, crushing everyone he said he loved—wives, sons, brothers, grandfathers, friends. No one was safe from his paranoid genocide—including thousands who resisted his take-over, dozens of the Sanhedrin (like the Supreme Court), and rabbis and their students defending God's Law.

"Evil is on the throne, and Israel has no hope," whispered the faithful Jews in Jerusalem.

When he sensed his own end was near, Herod filled Jericho's stadium with beloved countrymen with orders to kill everyone the moment he died—a sure way mourning would go global even if it wasn't for him.

If only character had matched his creative genius, Herod would have a respectable place in history. Yet today he's remembered only as the king who slaughtered babies in search of Jesus.

But don't think God is absent from any scene in history run by a madman. He is never more present than in evil's darkest hour.

On that night of nights, if Herod had only looked out his palace window—three miles southeast—he wouldn't have missed the star hovering over Bethlehem. He might have also wondered, *What's that light coming from shepherd's field? Is that singing?* In minutes, he could have walked his way to the manger and found Jesus.

But he didn't. Soon after, Herod's evil caught up with him, poisoning him, body, spirit, and soul. Gangrene ate his innards and his private parts rotted off. As he lay dying, his sanity unraveled like a cheap sweater.

Herod, the not so great after all.

Tomorrow: *One on one with the wise men*

Let's talk about it:

Every generation has its madmen.

1. What harm did Herod think Jesus was going to do to him?
2. How should we interpret political and cultural events in light of what we know about the spiritual dimension?
3. Herod was an Idumean, which means Esau was his ancestor. What insight does this lend to Herod's character.

DAY 20

Magi
The seekers who found Jesus

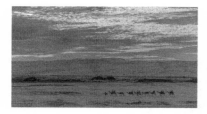

Now after Jesus was born in Bethlehem of Judea in the days of Herod the king, behold, wise men from the east came to Jerusalem, saying, "Where is he who has been born king of the Jews? For we saw his star when it rose and have come to worship him." Matthew 2:1-2

The fact that God sent them a personal invitation to the party is a truth we sometimes miss in all the attention on their extravagant gifts. That they came at all, traveling for more than a year across the desert to pay homage to a Jewish king, is reason enough to call them "wise." Others may call them something else to set out on such a journey with nothing more than a bright star to point the way.

When the wise men revealed God had written in the stars His announcement of the "new king of the Jews," it caused no small ruckus in the palace and around Jerusalem. Herod—near the end of his mad, mad life—couldn't contain his paranoia. After faking interest in worshipping this child, he shrewdly directed the visitors to Bethlehem (to find the child for him). Seems Herod's religious scholars knew all along that the Messiah would be born in Bethlehem but didn't bother to travel five miles down the road to investigate.

After their long, uncertain journey, the Magi were thrilled when the star appeared again, this time over the exact house where they would find Jesus.

Mary and Joseph must have been surprised (again) by the celebrity visitors at their door. The guests confirmed what Gabriel and Elizabeth and Simeon and the shepherds had all told them—that their miracle baby, Jesus, cutting His first tooth or taking His first steps by then, was the Messiah, sent by God on a rescue operation to save the world.

And if their Old Testament education served them right, the young couple also put two and two together that the magi's visit confirmed Isaiah's prophecy: Gentile nations would come and honor the Messiah. Their gifts of gold (for a king), frankincense (for worship), and myrrh (for burial) also foreshadowed Isaiah's suffering Servant.

As for the other questions (from what country did the Magi come and what exactly was that star?)—we just don't know. What we can say for sure is all the time we've focused on the unfolding drama in Israel, God was introducing characters in the spinoff series in another neighborhood on the other side of the world.

Gentiles, too, were looking for a Savior, and they traveled great lengths to follow every lead. And God, who promises to reward those who seek Him, used a star to signal them rescue was on the way.

Tomorrow: *One on one with refugees on the run*

Let's talk about it:

On a clear night, go outside and look at the stars. Psalm 19:1 says "the heavens are telling of the glory of God" God also uses His creation for special communication. Once a star was used as a special phenomenon, for a special time in history.

1. What does this miracle say about God's desire that Jesus birth be known to the world? A popular bumper sticker says "Wiseman still seek Him." What does this mean to you?
2. How do the gifts the Magi gave to Jesus reflect their understanding of who He really was? Practically speaking how might these gifts have been God's provision for the emergency trip the young family would take to Egypt

DAY 21

Refugees in Egypt
The unexpected way home

Then Herod, when he saw that he had been tricked by the wise men, became furious, and he sent and killed all the male children in Bethlehem and in all that region who were two years old or under. Matthew 2:16

Like refugees running from terrorists, Joseph snuck his young family out of Bethlehem in the middle of the night with nothing but dark, dangerous miles ahead.

Again, an angel had met Joseph in a dream and warned him of Herod's troops on their way to Bethlehem, intent on massacring every baby boy in the neighborhood, hoping the baby Messiah would be one of them.

Joseph and Mary took only what they could carry. She bundled up Jesus against the night air and away from the eyes of curious spies. Joseph likely grabbed the gifts the wise men had just given them. They were out of their house by daybreak.

The dawn would bring unspeakable grief to the sleepy towns around Bethlehem. Because of Joseph's quick obedience to God's warning, the three of them escaped by just hours.

Where do you run when the king wants your baby dead? Their only option was Egypt, barely outside the madman's reach. Just seventy-five miles to the border along the Via Maris (the ancient road called, "The Way of the Sea") and then another 200 miles to the nearest town. Before they could rest again, they would walk the better part of two weeks. Once out of harm's way, they hid out as fugitives inside Jewish communities either in Alexandria or Heliopolis in Egypt's northern delta.

What a detour <sigh>—one more for Mary and Joseph in a year already packed with highjacked plans. Their hopes for a quiet life in Nazareth had taken one dramatic turn after another. In retrospect, this detour shaped their young lives—what often happens to us, too, when life changes direction. Look what we can learn from their choices:

1. **Before doing anything, listen for God's direction.** Joseph had learned to recognize God's voice. Three times he trusted and obeyed, following the angel's orders in each difficult or dangerous case.
2. **Then, respond with courage rooted in faith in God.** Barely starting out in life, Mary too had proven she would respond bravely if she knew God was in it. Now, faith allowed them to act fast when confronted with the unthinkable.
3. **Understand there's a bigger plan in play.** Not only did this detour into Egypt fulfill the prophecy in Hosea 11:1 that God would call His Son out of Egypt, it also proved to Joseph and Mary how God would protect and provide for them in every emergency. Something bigger is always in the works.

If we're honest, most of us could point to detours in our lives. Looking back with faith, we sometimes see the unexpected way was

59

the best route after all. The detour is a mystery, but trusting God is always the safest way home.

Tomorrow: *One on one with Jesus as a toddler*

 Let's talk about it:

In recent years, the news is full of stories of families who have needed to run from danger.

1. Do you think Joseph and Mary were courageous or paranoid?
2. What unexpected things happened for their family that fulfilled God's plan?
3. How have you seen God use the "detours" in your life to bring you to where you are today with Him?

DAY 22

Jesus as a toddler
with the Word became flesh

And the Word became flesh and dwelt among us, and we have seen his glory, glory as of the only Son from the Father, full of grace and truth.
John 1:14

In those first years when the spring rains filled the Galilee countryside with poppies and the days grew noticeably longer, did Mary get nostalgic and tell Jesus His birth story as she tucked Him into bed at night?

"It was in the Spring when we traveled all the way to Bethlehem to register for taxes and I was as big as a donkey . . ." And likely little Jesus giggled, His dark eyes dancing.

"And we bedded down in the stable area, with nothing but a lantern to light our faces." (She left out the part about how alone they felt, and the stable's stench . . . and how she fought against the fear. I kept remembering Gabriel's words, "Do not fear, Mary, God is with you...").

"And then," she tickled her boy, "there you were, all wiggly and slippery in our arms. You were the most perfect baby in the world. How many lambies—one, two, three, four, five, six, seven, eight, nine, ten toes." He squealed as she pulled off his sandals. "Ah, Jesus," (cuddling now), "You were better than our hopes—better than our dreams for generations and generations since Father Abraham.

"I wish your grandparents could have been there." Her voice trailed off. "They would have been so proud. And the neighbors, oh, they would have thrown you a party and sung blessings to us outside our window."

"What else, Ama? What else happened?" the little guy probably begged, even with every detail memorized.

"Well, we had company." Her eyes twinkled. "Abba and I had barely cleaned you up when through the gate burst the most charming band of shepherds, awkwardly polite with big eyes."

"And sheep?!"

"Just one or two lambs in their arms. It was Spring; their sheep were in pasture."

"And what did they say?"

"The oddest thing—they said they came to see You for themselves. They had been in the field minding their business when a swarm of angels appeared out of nowhere in bright lights and lots of shouting. They were so scared. And they said, all on top of each another, 'the spirit said a child was born and He would bless the world. And we'd find Him sleeping in a trough. And there He is, just like they said.' "And Abba talked with them outside in the moonlight and explained some of the wonderful things the angels had told us."

"Like what, Ama?"

"Like, You are a special boy who will grow up to save our people. My little *Mashiach* . . . my Chosen One. You are God with us." With His head resting on her shoulder, she hummed a lullaby.

You have to wonder if in the dark of that evening, Mary looked out the window at the Milky Way chasing our tiny blue planet. Did she know this mystery tucked beneath her roof had named each star? And even that moment held the universe together?

The Light of the world stepped into darkness and we beheld His glory.

The Word became flesh and dwelt among us. And she held Him in her lap and taught Him

His A-B-C's.

Tomorrow: *One on one with Jesus—20 questions*

 Let's talk about it:

We know very little about Jesus' formulative years. But with God's completed Word in our hands, we know much more than Mary ever did.

1. What one fact about Jesus do you return to again and again in your faith journey?
2. Read Colossians 1:15-20. How does this picture of toddler Jesus fit with the description of Jesus' life and purpose in Colossians 1:15-20?

■■ DAY 23 ■■

20 Questions for Jesus
What would you ask Him?

And [Jesus] grew and became strong; he was filled with wisdom, and the grace of God was on him. Luke 2:40

1. What's your earliest memory? Mary's voice? Playing with James? Or do you remember angels?

2. Who were your best friends when you were 10 . . . 18 . . . 25?

3. Did you ever catch Mary looking hard at you while you played? Did your Aunt Elizabeth or Uncle Zechariah whisper as they watched you? Did they treat you differently?

4. Were you close to your cousin John when you were boys?

5. Did you wear a phylactery? Did you get excited every time to see the temple in Jerusalem?

6. Who was your favorite patriarch? King David? Or maybe Isaac . . .?

7. Do you resemble anyone in your family?

8. Which hill was your favorite to wander? . . . east to Mount Tabor where you stood with Moses and Elijah? . . . west looking at the Mediterranean glisten in the sun? . . . south toward Megiddo where armies marched through history. . . and where you will one day ride into the Valley of Armageddon? . . . or did you look further south to Jerusalem and to another hill?

9. Which of Mary's homemade dishes brought you home the quickest?

10. What family tradition quieted you? Passover or Yom Kippur—Atonement Day?

11. Did you ever comfort the Passover lamb before you spilt its blood?

12. How old were you when Joseph died? How did you feel at his funeral?

13. Did you whistle while you worked at your craft? Did you enjoy the people you met and worked with in Sephoris? Did you sit at night with the other men in the gates of Nazareth?

14. When you visited Jerusalem for feast days, did you ever see a crucifixion?

15. Did you ever wish to stay in Nazareth? Settle down, raise a family?

16. Did you miss your Heavenly Father? How did you cope with the humility of humanity?

17. Did 30 years seem like a moment . . . or an eternity?

18. What did you pray about that no one else knew?

19. How did you know it was time to leave?

20. Did you ever think of me?

Tomorrow: *One on one with Jesus in His hometown*

 Let's talk about it:

1. If Jesus sat across from you right now, what would you like to ask Him?
2. What do you think He'd ask you?

DAY 24

Nazareth

The town behind the scenes

Then he went down to Nazareth with them and was obedient to them. But his mother treasured all these things in her heart. And Jesus grew in wisdom and stature, and in favor with God and man. Luke 2:51-52

A shoot will come up from the stump of Jesse; from his roots a Branch will bear fruit. Isaiah 11:1

It's an understatement to say Jesus grew up in a small country town. Nazareth, then home to no more than 300 people, felt like a first-century diner and gas truck stop. The hometown God chose for His Son sat on a hill just north of the "freeway"—the trade route moving an endless caravan of creaking wagons across the Middle East. A military outpost camped nearby. Jesus grew up with the rough and tumble people from all over the ancient world.

No wonder Nathanael curled his lip when he first heard of "Jesus of Nazareth." *Can anything good come out of there?*

On any given day, Jesus spoke Aramaic with a Galilean accent and Hebrew in the synagogue. He picked up Greek from neighbors and traders. Jesus could talk to virtually anyone in their heart language.

Like other boys with their dads, Jesus learned Joseph's trade—a *tekton*, often translated "carpenter." Literally, a *tekton* is "a craftsman who builds" and since Israel's towns were built of rock, Jesus likely worked not with wood, but with stone. He may have even helped build nearby Sepphoris, a city with modern streets, a theatre, and gymnasium all under construction when Jesus lived in Nazareth.

As towns go, Nazareth was as ordinary as they come, but its origin has a telling little secret. Jews coming home from Babylon settled Nazareth about 100 years before Jesus lived there. They called it their family name, Natsar. The Natsoreans, meaning "branch," linked themselves with God's promise to David, believing Messiah, "the Branch," would be born from their family. To Jews in more cultured cities, the Natsoreans must have seemed hill-billy-silly in their assumed self-importance.

Matthew says of Jesus, "He shall be called a Nazarene"—more likely a "Natsarene," the secret hidden in the reversal of one letter, the difference between the Hebrew and Greek spelling. Natsarene says Jesus is a "branch from Jesse," from David's family (fulfilling Isaiah 11:1)—one more picture of Messiah fulfilled in Jesus.

As it does today, life revealed itself in first century Nazareth in the day by day normalcy. But behind the scenes, God's mysteries unfolded—hiding the precious in the ordinary. One day, purposefully and in proper time, the world was let in on the secret of who Jesus is and what He came to do.

Makes you wonder—what story is God writing in the details of your seemingly ordinary life? Time will tell.

Tomorrow: *One on one with Jesus—what would His mother say?*

Let's talk about it:

When you grow up in a small town or any close-knit community, for better or worse you know people as they know you.

1. As Jesus grew up, how do you think God use the climate of His hometown to prepare Him for ministry?
2. Do you know what it's like to come from a hometown with a bad reputation? How does it shape your character?

DAY 25

Mary, interviewed
The mom who treasured Jesus

Then he went down to Nazareth with them and was obedient to them. But his mother treasured all these things in her heart. And Jesus grew in wisdom and stature, and in favor with God and man. Luke 2:51-52

[Imagine the Gospel writer, Luke's interview with Mary—part 1]
Thank you for sharing your story with us, Mary. No one can tell us about Jesus better than you, the one God chose to be His mother. Recently, some have taught Jesus was human, but not God. Others say the opposite—that He was God, but not human. What do you say to that?

Mary: [laughing] Well, as the one who bore Him, burped Him, and changed His soiled diapers, and...and sat across from Him at the evening meal for almost thirty years, I can tell you for certain Jesus is human.

And also, I will tell you He is God. I know better than anyone Jesus was conceived by the Holy Spirit. But I also followed Jesus as rabbi. I saw His miracles, heard Him teach. I stood with Him at that wretched cross and I saw Him again, alive, days later. I know better than anyone He is God Himself.

Yes, He is both. Now I'm old and can see my life better. I remember things He said and did—moments that stole my heart long before He captured anyone else's. I hold every memory—even those things I don't understand. Like the old man in the temple, what he said. For years I suffered night terrors as Jesus slept safely under our roof.

Yes, Jesus certainly is a man. By day, He worked hard—in the shop, or in Sephoris or Tiberius—both towns boomed with work when we lived in Nazareth. Of course, Jesus was Nazareth's most eligible bachelor. How many mothers asked me, "So, isn't it time for Jesus to pick a wife?" [Laughs.]

Dinner was fun for us with nieces and nephews competing for Jesus' attention or His brothers picking His brain on some problem. Often the men from synagogue dropped by to talk to Jesus, and they would sit under the stars and debate some line from Torah. And while the girls and I finished the chores, I eavesdropped and smiled when Jesus' calm questions would settle their nerves . . . or sometimes stir up new questions.

What's a favorite memory from that time?

Sabbat. Every Friday night. When I lit the Sabbat candles, work stopped. We lingered at the table, warmed with good things to eat and each other's company. And we talked of God's goodness. The candles glowed on my children's faces and the grandchildren quieted and cuddled. Someone would retell a family story and we laughed. Or remember something about Joseph, and our eyes would moisten.

Jesus was the patriarch for those years. That is, until it was time for Him to go. Somehow He knew when.

If I sit quiet, sometimes I think I still hear His voice, *Mommy, help me lace my sandals? Mom, what's for dinner? Woman, don't you know My time is not yet come? Dear Mother, behold your son . . . Mom, I'll be back.*

Tomorrow: *One on one with Mary—on the day they lost Him*

 Let's talk about it:

1. If you're a mom, or you grew up with a mom, what details do you remember about your family when they were young? How would this be same/different for Mary?
2. How does time help clarify?

DAY 26

Parents
The day they lost Jesus

Every year Jesus' parents went to Jerusalem for the Festival of the Passover. When he was twelve years old, they went up to the festival, according to the custom. After the festival was over, while his parents were returning home, the boy Jesus stayed behind in Jerusalem, but they were unaware of it. Luke 2:41-43

[Imagine the Gospel writer, Luke's interview with Mary, part 2]

If there is one story to tell about Jesus' boyhood, what would you share?

Mary: You probably want me to tell you about when we lost Jesus, right?

Whatever story you want...

Mary: Very well. Crazy, isn't it? Joseph thought He was with me and the other children. I thought He was with Joseph. Jesus was a

73

good boy—no mischief, no trouble. Even at 12, we could trust Him. When He wasn't with me, I thought, "So this is the trip Jesus walks with the men. Good for Him."

Of course, we turned back to Jerusalem the moment we realized He wasn't with either of us. Can you believe it? The God of the universe entrusts us with this special boy, and we lose Him! Such a sick panic in my heart for three days.

Well, you know the story—we found Him with the rabbis on Temple Mount. Jesus looked up at us like it was nothing. Not a bit of worry or remorse, even when I gave Him a piece of my mind. I knew Him better than anyone, and I realized in that moment, I didn't know Him at all.

"Don't you know I'm to do my Father's business?" He said and everyone who heard, especially Joseph—knew He wasn't talking about being a craftsman in Nazareth. If Joseph was hurt, he didn't let on.

That was the day Jesus grew from a boy to a man. A man on a mission. That was the day Joseph and I knew the secret we had kept all these years was out. Jesus was here for more.

He came back with us to Nazareth and was as obedient as always. He grew so tall and strong. His mind was brilliant and His spirit alive. People loved Him. . . . God's hand was on Him.

But from then on, Jesus' focus was somewhere else. Sometimes I watched Him from the shadows when He stood alone in His workshop or with the *tallit* over His head as He prayed. I watched Him return from the hills where He would walk before dawn. I just knew He was talking to His Father about the days to come. I fought the rush of time. *Not yet, Jesus, not yet.*

It was beyond us, I knew that. But for a short lifetime, I got to play my part in something bigger than the universe. I didn't even know how big. Jesus came for more.

Tomorrow: *One on one with the Light of the world*

Let's talk about it:

Mary and Joseph were people just like us. Remember that as you read the Christmas story.

1. How do you think Mary felt to be chosen for such an amazing responsibility?
2. How does knowing that Luke one into you were influenced by Mary's memories personalize the account for you

DAY 27

The Light

The One who is with us

Then came the Festival of Dedication at Jerusalem. It was winter, and Jesus was in the temple courts walking in Solomon's Colonnade. The Jews who were there gathered around him, saying, "How long will you keep us in suspense? If you are the Messiah, tell us plainly." John 10:22-24

When the first twinkling lights show up in December, a magical, meaningful season begins.

The boy Jesus would have loved the holidays as much as we do. When Mary lit the candles for Hanukkah, picture Him staring at the menorah, excited each evening to light one candle after another until all eight candles flickered in the darkness. Less than 200 years earlier, God had rescued Israel from a Syrian takeover, and this sacred candelabra told the story of *"nes gadol haya sham,"* the great miracle that happened.

In 165 B.C. the Syrian king, Antiochus, took over Israel and demanded the Jews abandon God and His ways. He declared it illegal to read God's Word. Illegal to circumcise. Illegal to pray. To make sure no one could worship God in the temple, Antiochus sacrificed a pig on the altar.

The heroes of this generation were the Maccabees, a family of courageous priests who led the revolt against Syria. Tradition says in the middle of the take-back, they lit the sacred candelabra in the temple—a symbol of God's presence with them—and a day's worth of oil supernaturally burned for eight. The celebration commemorating the temple's re-dedication is called Hanukkah (dedication), the Festival of Lights.

Jesus celebrated Hanukkah His whole life. In John 10 we read He was in Jerusalem at the temple, celebrating the Festival of Light. No surprise—there was no other place He'd rather be for Hanukkah.

Jesus' arrival ended the 400 years the Jews had followed God in His silence. The menorah's light reminded them of God's promise, "I will be with you." In that holy season, Jerusalem was lit up like a Christmas tree.

When John in his gospel described how Jesus came into the world, he didn't talk about the manger or the angels or a star, but instead he wrote, *in Jesus was life, and that life was the light of all mankind.*

How oddly beautiful it must have been for Jesus, fully God and fully man, to see the lit menorah blazing in the night and remember when as Creator, He spoke the world out of darkness. *"Let there be light"* and there was.

Or to remember how for forty years in the wilderness, night after night, He was with His people as a pillar of fire, a flame to light the way. For more than 14,000 nights He reminded them, "you're not alone in this darkness. *I am with you."*

He told the Maccabees the same message in the oil that didn't run out. *I am still with you.*

The same thing He tells us when by faith we stand like a candle against a dark world, *I am with you.* Even today, there's no other place He'd rather be than with us.

Tomorrow: *One on one with Jesus, why He came*

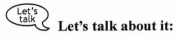 **Let's talk about it:**

The miracle of Hanukkah's oil lamp is like your phone's battery at 1% lasting for eight days.

1. By any chance, do you have a personal symbol of God's presence with you? Why is it meaningful to you?
2. Sometime when you're alone, or scared, or anxious, repeat His promise to yourself, "I am with you." How/why does that help?

DAY 28

The Why

The reason behind the story

For God so loved the world that he gave his one and only Son, that whoever believes in him shall not perish but have eternal life. For God did not send his Son into the world to condemn the world, but to save the world through him. John 3:16-17

All things considered, the Bible doesn't give us much details about Christmas. Instead, and even better than details, God's Word tells us the "why" behind the story.

The greatest fact is that Jesus came at all.[1] The second greatest fact is that He invites you to come to Him.

O, come all ye faithful. Joyful and triumphant . . . and everyone else, too. If you walk in darkness but long for light. If you will take a chance at believing something beyond proving. If you will take a step closer and let God whisper into your ear . . . . . *I love you*—that's the why of Christmas.

GOD LOVED THE WORLD SO MUCH THAT HE GAVE HIS ONLY SON, SO THAT EVERYONE WHO BELIEVES IN HIM SHALL NOT BE LOST, BUT HAVE ETERNAL LIFE. [2]

God loves you like a groom loves his bride,[3] like a father loves his child,[4] like an artist loves his masterpiece.[5]

No one knows you better—all your secrets, and faults, all the peculiarities only a Lover knows.[6] Yet His love doesn't depend on how beautiful you are, but on how beautiful He is. His affection for you is not at risk when you fail at your job or your marriage or your life—because His love never depended on you in the first place. He loves you because that's what He is.[7]

Jesus is love come down. To earth. To us.

Like a magnet, His love pulls you to Him.

So, come, all you faithful. Come to Jesus.

Look closely enough and you'll find He's better than you thought and more than you hoped He'd be.

In Him appeared life and this life was the light of mankind. The Light still shines in the darkness and the darkness has never put it out. [8]

He's light to you when you grope in the dark.

He's love—the kind you've longed for and never dreamed existed.

This is the "why" He's come.

[1]John 10:10 [2]John 3:16 [3]Song of Sol. 4:10 [4]Ps. 103:13 [5]Eph. 2:10 [6]Ps. 139:3 [7]1 Jn. 4:16 7 [8]John 1:5

Tomorrow: *One on one with Jesus when God says "now"*

 Let's talk about it:

1. Read over the eight verses referenced in this devotional. Which one speaks most to you? Why? Memorize one.
2. Have you ever felt God's love draw you like a magnet? Describe it.
3. Is Jesus your Savior? How do you know?

DAY 29

The Perfect Moment
When God says 'now'

But when the set time had fully come, God sent his Son, born of a woman, born under the law, to redeem those under the law, that we might receive adoption to sonship. Galatians 4:4-5

The world holds its breath this week. These are the days "in-between"—a hinge between the year that will soon end, and the one waiting to start.

Time is on our minds today—how quickly it passes, how to make the most of it, how not to run out of it before, you know, it's your time.

Look closely at Advent and you'll see time tracks between every line. Galatians 4:4 says Jesus came "when time was full"—meaning, *"When days and events had run their course, salvation emerged on the human scene— God's plan reached the precise moment when Jesus arrived in Mary's womb."*

Jesus entered time and space at the perfect moment in history.

We might have picked a later date when conditions were more sanitary, or when more people could have heard Jesus firsthand through mass media . . . or when crucifixion was out of style. But Jesus was born right on time, in perfect synch with His purposes. God braided one era into the next, weaving people and events together in a beautiful cord. Even the powers of darkness couldn't hinder God's plan.

Think about that as you review your life this past year. God has been at work—behind every scene, shaping every nuance of every event. Even today, things are being crafted to fit together according to His purposes. That is always God's way (called "sovereignty").

But wait, you say. *Something in my life feels overdue.* Or *sometimes I wonder what's ahead.* "Don't worry," God says. You can be sure there will yet be that perfect moment when His time is full and His very private, specific plan for your life will be accomplished. He is not slow. He won't forget. Even your dumb mistakes can't mess up what He has in mind for you.

So walk by faith into the new year. Keep following Jesus. Build bumpers in your life to accomplish that one thing. The word is *steadfast*—keep going in the same direction. And if you need to adjust, now is the perfect time.

As this season turns, remember God's purposes are stirring in our generation, on your street, in your heart. Hold your breath and stay alert. Something's about to happen, something holy and precious and beyond words is seeking to be born, even in us. Even this year.

Tomorrow: *One on one with Jesus in the new year*

 Let's talk about it:

1. What bumpers can you build in your life to make sure you keep on following Jesus? Describe them.
2. How has God been at work in your life this year?
3. What do you think God's specific plan for your life includes? How is it same/different from other generations'?

DAY 30

Next Year
Walk with Jesus in the new year

All these people were still living by faith when they died. They did not receive the things promised; they only saw them and welcomed them from a distance, admitting that they were foreigners and strangers on earth. People who say such things show that they are looking for a country of their own. If they had been thinking of the country they had left, they would have had opportunity to return. Instead, they were longing for a better country—a heavenly one. Therefore God is not ashamed to be called their God, for he has prepared a city for them. Hebrews 11:13-16

And so the greatest story in history has begun.

We visited the people and the places surrounding Jesus' arrival on earth and into our story—or should we say, our chapter in God's story. His is the bigger narrative—the meta-narrative of life and death, of strength and beauty, of choice and will, happening according to His timing and accomplishing His plan. For history. For you.

Did you recognize yourself between the lines of the Christmas story? No matter where you are today, you can take heart in what God says about people like us.

- *Questioning what God is doing?* Remember Joseph and Zechariah.
- *Waiting—for what seems like a lifetime?* Remember Elizabeth and Simeon and Anna.
- *Looking for God in a confusing culture?* Remember the shepherds and the Magi.
- *Willing to do what God asks if He would just show you how?* Remember Mary and John.

Trusting God ties the whole story together. *Will I trust Him with the details of my life? No matter how crazy that feels? Will I ask Him for faith to believe He's at work? Will I listen for His voice?* Those are your questions to answer.

In Part 2 of *One on One with Jesus*, you will meet Jesus in His one-on-one encounters with people who look and act a lot like us. How will He touch them? How will their lives change? What can we learn about God's big story touching us today?

Walk with Jesus in the new year and find out.

 Let's talk about it:

1. Which of the people you met in this first part of Jesus' story do you resonate with most? Why?
2. Dream a little. What story is God writing in the details of your seemingly ordinary life?
3. What would you like your story to be?

PART 2

ONE ON ONE WITH JESUS – IN HIS MINISTRY YEARS

First there was Bethlehem, and now, 30 years have gone by. Jesus is an itinerant teacher on the road—a road eventually taking Him to Jerusalem and the reason He came in the first place. To be clear, He came to be with us. He moved into the neighborhood so we could someday be with Him in His neighborhood. In these 35 days, we'll walk with Jesus on the streets of Jerusalem and the villages of Galilee as He meets people as they are, one on one.

PART 2
One on One with Jesus – in His Ministry Years

DAY 1

In the Neighborhood
The One who lives down the street

The Word became flesh and made his dwelling among us. We have seen his glory, the glory of the one and only Son, who came from the Father, full of grace and truth. John 1:14

First there was Bethlehem, and now, 30 years have gone by. Turn the page and Jesus is a middle-aged man, working for a living in northern Israel. He's active in the synagogue, respected by the community, and the patriarch of His family. The Gospels pick up here in Jesus' life as He begins His ministry as an itinerant teacher on the road—a road that eventually leads to Jerusalem and the reason He came in the first place.

To be clear, He came to be with us. Turns out Isaiah's prophecy was spot on. Jesus is *Immanuel*—God with us. Literally, He moved into the neighborhood. His reason for coming? So we could someday be with Him in His neighborhood.

Here is where our days of *One on One with Jesus in Ministry* begins. The *with* says it all. When you walk *with* someone, you tend not to be in such a hurry. Conversations come more relaxed. We'll walk with Jesus as He talks with people one on one on the streets of Jerusalem and in the villages of Galilee. Each person feels like He's intentionally penciled in a meeting with them on His calendar.

Just ask anyone in Galilee and they likely heard of Jesus. In these three years, He's the famous, hometown boy: Jesus—the next-door Savior who captured the heart of a nation.

Those whom Jesus touched would just tell you how He loved them, simple as that. To hear Him teach captured their attention. And to hear Him pray? It was like He was right there in heaven talking to His dad. No one ever prayed like that before.

They watched Jesus grow up so they knew He was human but could He also be the promised Messiah—the Christ, right under their noses? That question swirled wherever He went. *Yes, perhaps He could be Messiah*, many thought—but not like they were expecting. Nothing about Jesus was as they expected.

No one expected the wind to listen when He said "hush." Or for thousands to be fed from a boy's lunch of fish and crackers. Or for bodies ravaged by severed spinal cords, detached retinas, and ovarian cancer to be made whole in a snap. No one dreamed their dead child would again sit beside them at the supper table and laugh and snort milk out their nose.

To be honest, no one expected this Messiah would really see them—the lost, the wounded, the one barely hanging on. But He did see them. Imagine that—He still does.

Because He came to be with us. One on one.

Tomorrow: *One on one with Jesus in the water*

 Let's talk about it:

1. What do you hope to learn or experience as you discover more about Jesus' ministry years?
2. Do you think Jesus sees you?

DAY 2

Water

The One who identifies with us

Then Jesus came from Galilee to the Jordan to be baptized by John. But John tried to deter him, saying, "I need to be baptized by you, and do you come to me?"

Jesus replied, "Let it be so now; it is proper for us to do this to fulfill all righteousness." Then John consented. As soon as Jesus was baptized, he went up out of the water. At that moment heaven was opened, and he saw the Spirit of God descending like a dove and alighting on him. And a voice from heaven said, "This is my Son, whom I love; with him I am well pleased." Matthew 3:13-17

After the fanfare with His birth settled down, Jesus grew up in Nazareth, a quiet ninety miles from Jerusalem. How Jesus knew when it was time to go public, no one knows.

Maybe Jesus knew His time had come when rumors spread that in the desert, John was preaching about the coming kingdom of God.

Or maybe Jesus' spiritual hearing was so keen He heard His Father whisper, "*now*." So, at just the right time and for the last time, Jesus pulled the door shut to His shop and set off to see John.

Down in Judea where the Jordan River met the wilderness, John "the Baptizer" was making quite a ruckus about how people should relate to God. "Your Jewish-ness isn't your ticket to heaven," he preached. "Only an honest turn from sin will open your heart to God. Only then will you be ready for the Messiah."

As he described what this Messiah will be and do and say, the religious in the crowd got hotter and the repentant in the crowd got in the water, asking to be baptized. Down into the water as a picture of washing away their sin, then raised face-first from the rushing current with eyes focused on their new life in God.

One day from out of the crowd on the shore, Jesus Himself stepped into the water. When John saw Him there, he shouted to everyone, "Here He is! The One who will take away your sin. He's the One I've been telling you about; He's the Passover Lamb of God!"

Then Jesus asked John for an unexplainable thing—to be baptized, too. John objected, "You? You don't need to repent!" but the Lord insisted. "Let it be this way . . ."

The picture became clearer with the years; just as Jesus would someday die for us so we could be forgiven, Jesus came out of the water, a Savior. Right on mission, He did what His Father asked. He who *had never* and *would never* sin, obeyed as if He was a sinner so we could be treated as if we were not.

When Jesus' face emerged out of the water, eyes towards the sky, His Father did a beautiful thing—He broke into time and space with a message for His Son. John later told anyone who would listen, "When I saw the Spirit come down like a dove and land on Jesus . . . we heard this voice out of the blue say, *My Son, I am so delighted in You and what You are doing.'* I knew, I just knew. Jesus is the One."

After thirty years away, the sound of His Father's affirming voice must have felt a little like heaven for Him. And that's good—because Jesus would cover a lot of ground before He would see heaven again.

Tomorrow: *One on one with Jesus in the desert*

 Let's talk about it:

1. Have you been baptized? What does being baptized mean to you?
2. Do you agree or disagree with John's phrase, "Only an honest turn from sin will open your heart to God."

DAY 3

960 Hours
The One who chose you

Jesus, full of the Holy Spirit, left the Jordan and was led by the Spirit into the wilderness, where for forty days he was tempted by the devil. He ate nothing during those days, and at the end of them he was hungry.
Luke 4:1-3

Forty days is a long time. Ask any recovering alcoholic and they'll tell you before you claim victory *one day at a time*, you must resist the temptation to drink one *hour* at a time. Even one *moment* at a time.

Overcoming the temptation to sin is a battle of moments for all of us.

Today we're with Jesus in a place He spent more than three and a half *million* moments being tempted by the devil. Gone are the green hills of Jesus' northern country. This is His cousin John's land. Desolate. Rugged. Undulating heat. No water or trees for miles. The wilderness is an unforgiving land.

Jesus had just been with John at the Jordan. Rising from the rushing water, the baptized Jesus heard His Father's voice, *"My Son, whom I love; with You I am well pleased."* From this high watermark, the Spirit led Jesus into the desert.

Greater than the heat and the silence of the wilderness, the stark reality of His humanity must have felt oppressive for Jesus. Sunburned and sand-whipped, His body ached with hunger. His tongue swelled with thirst. He was alone.

But not completely.

It's been ages since Jesus and Satan had been together last—an eternity past when Satan, as an angel in Jesus' service, was called "the son of the morning." Satan remembered those glory days. And he remembered Jesus in His glory.

You can have it again, he taunted. *Right now.* Perhaps the deceiver even used what sounded like the Father's voice, *Go ahead Son; You deserve the glory . . .*

Jesus could have chosen glory. He could have made a loaf of bread from a rock. He could have commanded angels to rescue Him. But He chose life instead. *Your* life. He couldn't accept Satan's attractive offer and be your Savior, too.

So, He chose you.

And in His choice, He earned the right to be your Advocate. Your high priest who identifies with your weakness. Someone who has been tempted in every way you are, yet without sinning.

What temptation beats on you today? Are you hungry for something which should be yours? Are you strategizing how God's will could be done sooner . . . or easier? Even Jesus must have agonized in the battle; it wouldn't have been a real test if He didn't. When it was over, He was so beat up that His Father dispatched angels to help Him.

Because Jesus spent those 960 hours in the wilderness, we have a way out of it. We can ask for help. We can get mercy in the exact moment we need it. When we're tempted to sin. When we're beat down. When we wish there was another way out. Jesus, now personally qualified and credible, gives us the strength to say no. The mercy to walk away. The grace to keep following after God. Just like He did.

Tomorrow: *One on one with Jesus at a wedding*

 Let's talk about it:

1. What do you think was Jesus' greatest temptation in Luke 4:1-13? To satisfy His hunger/thirst? To prove that He was God? To get the glory now?
2. What truth about sin/temptation will you take from this account of Jesus' experience?

DAY 4

Wine

The One who showed us His glory

Jesus said to the servants, "Fill the jars with water"; so they filled them to the brim. Then he told them, "Now draw some out and take it to the master of the banquet." They did so, and the master of the banquet tasted the water that had been turned into wine. He did not realize where it had come from, though the servants who had drawn the water knew. Then he called the bridegroom aside and said, "Everyone brings out the choice wine first and then the cheaper wine after the guests have had too much to drink; but you have saved the best till now." John 2:7-10

The last time we saw Jesus, He was a sunburnt, wind-whipped, starving, victorious warrior—walking out of earth's most treacherous landscape after forty days of fasting. But that wasn't even the worst of it. At His most vulnerable, Jesus fought Satan one on one for the right to be our Savior. It was an intense spiritual, physical, emotional, psychological battle and Jesus won hands-down. Satan limped away, mumbling something about a rematch.

<Deep breath. Exhale.>

Where do you go after such a trial? The best shelter is the company of people who love you. So Jesus went home to Galilee. It just so happened He arrived in time for a family wedding.

Weddings were a community event in Jesus' day. They began at night when the groom shows up at his bride's house and escorts her back to his family's home, parading through town so everyone can congratulate them and follow them back for a party—a party that lasts for days when the music plays and the food and the wine flows.

Except when it doesn't. That was the problem we hear about from Jesus' mother, Mary, who had some kind of responsibility at the party. She turns to her always-reliable Jesus. *"Son, the wine is gone! Do something!"*

Picture Jesus—lounging at the table, having a great time, full of life and love for the people around Him. In days to come whenever He wasn't preaching or teaching, you could find Jesus at some kind of gathering. The Pharisees criticized Him for enjoying Himself too much.

At first, Jesus objects to Mary's pleading, but something in His tone told her He'd help. He cared about what troubled her—even a social faux pas like this. One look in her anxious face, another look at the disciples watching Him, and Jesus steps into His new role of miracle-worker.

He told the staff to fill six large empty barrels with water—the thirty gallon kind used for ceremonial hand-washing. Then, he told them to take a sample to the wedding host. Somewhere between those two instructions, without any big show, the water became wine. Imagine the staff's surprise!

(By the way, if you do the math— 6 barrels x 30 gallons = 180 gallons of wine. In today's economy, if one bottle costs $30, then this was $27,000 worth of wine.)

When the master of ceremonies praised the host, imagine the sparkle in Jesus' eyes when He looked into the shocked faces of His mom and then the disciples and finally, the servants. It's enough to make Him throw back His head and laugh.

Yes, the best is yet to come.

Tomorrow: *One on one with Jesus on a sleepless night*

 Let's talk about it:

1. At first Jesus resisted Mary's request to help but then performed a miracle. "He cared about what troubled her." Do you believe Jesus cares about what troubles you?
2. Do you believe "the best is yet to come"?

DAY 5

Sleepless

The One who prays

One of those days Jesus went out to a mountainside to pray, and spent the night praying to God. When morning came, he called his disciples to him and chose twelve of them, whom he also designated apostles: Simon (whom he named Peter), his brother Andrew, James, John, Philip, Bartholomew, Matthew, Thomas, James son of Alphaeus, Simon who was called the Zealot, Judas son of James, and Judas Iscariot, who became a traitor. Luke 6:12-16

If you've ever stayed awake all night, you know the strange stillness that blankets a sleeping world.

What keeps you up all night? A red-eye flight. A sick child. Worry about a marriage or a mortgage, a diagnosis or a decision? This space in-between is a time to toss-and-turn—or a turning point, depending on how you spend those hours in the dark.

Jesus was up all night the day before He chose His twelve disciples. Imagine Him in moonlight, walking the hills around the Sea of Galilee, praying.

What do you think He prayed about?

Maybe Jesus rehearsed the candidates with His Father. These disciples would not only walk beside Him during the next three years, but it would be through their ministries the Gospel would spread to the world and the future church would learn and grow. They would become His spokesmen, His ambassadors.

Perhaps in His humanity, Jesus struggled with choices. *A zealot and a tax collector in the same group? Quiet Andrew? Thomas will doubt. And about Judas . . .*

Or He could have been praying for those who wouldn't be chosen. Or maybe He talked with His Father about something totally different . . . about another sleepless night He'll spend in a garden three years from now.

No wonder Jesus was up, asking for clarity, needing to feel connected to His Father, wanting to do His will. Somewhere under the stars, Jesus found resolve.

Before the sun peeked over the horizon, before the birds signaled the dawn, before the breeze carried the scent of thyme and sage across the lakeside, Jesus chose His team.

Sleepless nights are no stranger to God. The Psalmist says *He who keeps Israel will neither slumber nor sleep. The LORD is your keeper . . .He will keep you from all evil; He will keep your life (121:4).*

So, rest easy, the Lord will stay up. In the future when your mind won't rest in those midnight hours, follow Jesus' example. Talk to your Father in the dark and quiet in-between. Then in the morning, go do what He says.

Tomorrow: *One on one with Jesus in His choice*

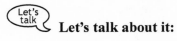 **Let's talk about it:**

1. When was the last time your thoughts kept you awake? How does Jesus' example inspire you?
2. How do you like to pray? Kneeling? Walking? Journaling? What are the pros/cons of the different ways?

DAY 6

Dusty
The One to follow

Anyone who loves their life will lose it, while anyone who hates their life in this world will keep it for eternal life. Whoever serves me must follow me; and where I am, my servant also will be. My Father will honor the one who serves me. John 12:25-26

You want to follow Jesus? You want to be like Him? Well, you're in good company. In first century Israel, true disciples also wanted to be like their rabbis and it started young.

From five-years old, a Jewish boy begins to read and memorize Scripture. By ten, he has memorized entire books of the Bible. By thirteen, if he shows interest in studying, he can go to Torah school at the local synagogue.

While most young men in Jesus' day married between fifteen and eighteen years old and began their life's work, the more gifted Bible students went deeper in their studies with an internship with an ordained rabbi, often traveling with him in an itinerant ministry.

These gifted students are called the rabbi's *talmidims*—his disciples. More than a student who wants to learn what a teacher *knows*, a talmidim wants *to be like* his teacher. He watches and listens and imitates his rabbi. He lives with him, picks up his mannerisms, and asks questions. Every rabbi had his own "yoke," his own way of following God. A disciple adopts his rabbi's yoke and would wear a WWJD bracelet if he could.

In Jesus' day, to follow a rabbi as a disciple meant to walk so closely in his footsteps that you are "covered with the dust of his feet."

Usually the disciple sought out the rabbi and asked to follow him; Jesus did it the other way around. He chose specific disciples to be with Him. He found His twelve students while they were fishing, collecting taxes, or praying and invited them, "Follow Me." They knew what it meant but maybe not yet what it would cost. John was probably the youngest (around fifteen)—Peter, who was married, and Matthew, already in a career, among the oldest.

So, for three years, Jesus' disciples followed Him without knowing where He was taking them. You don't ask, 'where are you taking us, Rabbi?' since following was part of the lesson. He would lead them to the right place for the lesson He wanted them to learn. One time, Jesus took them forty miles to ask them a single, specific question.

To follow Jesus today takes no less faith and maybe a little more. To follow means you know His yoke, you live by the rules of life that He models and tells you about in His Word. You follow even when you're not sure where He's taking you. You count the cost and want nothing more than to get your feet dusty, walking in His steps.

When Jesus says to you, "Follow Me," He opens a door and your whole life waits on the other side. *Come and see*, He says.

Tomorrow: *One on one with Jesus and His disciples*

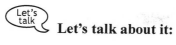 **Let's talk about it:**

1. What did you learn about being a disciple in today's reading? What truth resonated with you?

2. Do you think it takes more/less faith to follow Jesus today? Why?

DAY 7

Talmidim
The One worthy

For God so loved the world that he gave his one and only Son, that whoever believes in him shall not perish but have eternal life. For God did not send his Son into the world to condemn the world, but to save the world through him.
1 Corinthians 11:1

Lord Jesus,

When You chose Your disciples, You looked far down the road and saw not only who they were, but who they would be. Was it the same with me?

You knew when You said, "Follow Me," that they wouldn't sometimes. You knew how hard it would be for them to apply one day's miracle to the next day's crisis. Instead of it being maddening to You when they argued about who was the greatest (and didn't even mention You), You showed them what greatness looks like. You wrapped a towel around Your waist and washed their feet.

We easily give up on us. Some days we boast like clouds without rain. The thick-headed one who doesn't remember yesterday's miracle. The fearful one who lets a stranger carry Your cross.

Yet knowing all these things about us, You don't give up on us. You know after years of following You that some of Your dust will get on our feet. Some things true about You become true about us. And when people look at us, they see things that teach them about You.

These disciples gave their lives for You, short or long. Help me be like them when they were like You.

We want Peter's kind of passion, who raced to the tomb at the hint You could be alive again—and then ran hard after You for the rest of his life.

Like Andrew who lived forever in his brother Peter's shadow, yet every time we meet him, he's humble and unphased, bringing yet another person to You.

Like Thomas who let You confront his dark side, and then believed You. And didn't stop believing for the rest of his life, telling others about You who had not seen and yet still believed.

We want to be like John who stood by You at Your cross and for a lifetime after. Sixty years later, after everyone else from the team had died, he told the world about You so still more would believe.

And Nathanael, whose pure love for You was without strategy or shades of gray.

And Matthew, the sharp opportunist You rescued from an empty, money-hungry life—that's the kind of reversal we're after.

Even James who served You quietly—like the millions who have followed in behind-the-scenes service ever since. We want to follow You that way.

We want to give our lives to You, Lord Jesus. Not just in the doing, but in the being. Help us be Your disciple, Your *talmidim*, who follows not just Your teaching but Your life.

This we ask, because You love us to the uttermost. Amen.

Tomorrow: *One on one with Jesus and His cousin, John*

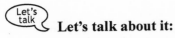 **Let's talk about it:**

1. Describe the difference between a student and a talmadim. Which do you want to be? How?
2. Which of the disciples do you identify with? In what way?

DAY 8

Expectations
The One who is greater

When John, who was in prison, heard about the deeds of the Messiah, he sent his disciples to ask him, "Are you the one who is to come, or should we expect someone else?" Jesus replied, "Go back and report to John what you hear and see: The blind receive sight, the lame walk, those who have leprosy are cleansed, the deaf hear, the dead are raised, and the good news is proclaimed to the poor.
Matthew 11:2-5

Jesus doesn't always meet our expectations.

John didn't expect to die that day in Herod's prison. He thought Jesus would get him out somehow. Didn't the prophet Isaiah say the Messiah would open prison doors and set the captives free? But weeks became months, and Jesus didn't come. And a fear gripped John the Baptist's heart that he had been wrong. That Jesus wasn't the One.

Only the proud would call John out on his doubt—or those who've never experienced a desperate prayer gone unanswered. A marriage doesn't survive. A depression doesn't lift. A wayward child doesn't return. A remission doesn't heal. Only those who have tasted that abandonment can sit with John in prison and wonder if Jesus is the Savior after all.

His whole life, the strong-hearted John knew his mission was to announce the Messiah—the angel Gabriel had told that to his parents. But now the "voice crying in the wilderness," cried out as an innocent man on death row. Did he get the message wrong? Is Jesus the Lamb of God?

So, John did the right thing with his doubt, he took it to Jesus Himself. On a day when Jesus stood before the crowds, teaching and healing and changing destinies, John's disciples interrupted, "John needs to know—are You the One, or do we look for another?"

Jesus hears their question but doesn't answer. He just keeps healing broken bodies and hearts. He leaves John's men waiting and watching. Then after who knows how long, He tells them, "Go tell John what you have seen and heard: . . . about the blind who now see and the paralyzed who now walk, about the broken-hearted who now sing, and the dead who live again." —all clues from the prophet Isaiah on how to recognize the coming Messiah.

So as one chapter begins, another ends. John's life, the bright, hot comet flying across the night sky, burns out in an obscure prison cell at the whim of a foolish girl, her resentful mother, and a wicked, weak king. We don't even know if John got Jesus' message.

But if John, now knowing the bigger story, could be a voice to us again, he would tell every broken-hearted follower of Jesus to keep believing. Even in your doubt. Even in the brunt of life's bitter blows. What's ahead is so much better than anything you're wishing for. Really.

Because when your expectation is tied to Jesus's bigger mission, your future reality will be better than anything you hope or pray for. Fix your eyes on Jesus and keep on. The joy is still ahead.

Tomorrow: *One on one with Jesus and Nicodemus*

Let's talk about it:

1. Most of us have doubted something about our faith. The real test is where you take your doubt. What has been your experience?

2. How have you seen the Lord overcome your doubt? How has He proved Himself worthy of your trust? Ask someone who's faith has been vibrant and long to tell you about their experience.

DAY 9

Wind

The One who moves like the wind

Now there was a Pharisee, a man named Nicodemus who was a member of the Jewish ruling council. [2] He came to Jesus at night and said, "Rabbi, we know that you are a teacher who has come from God. For no one could perform the signs you are doing if God were not with him." Jesus replied, "Very truly I tell you, no one can see the kingdom of God unless they are born again." "How can someone be born when they are old?" Nicodemus asked. John 3:1-4

Nicodemus was no coward. He didn't come at night to avoid being seen talking to the Teacher. He came at night because that's when us Jews love to talk. Under the stars, old men dream dreams, and young men see visions. And Pharisees debate about God.

I had followed the Rabbi two years when I met Nicodemus that night. Me, a talmidim from Galilee meeting a member of the Sanhedrin. What an honor! He looked me square in the face and asked, *Is what they say about your rabbi true? Does He raise the dead?* And I said, *I've seen it, sir.*

They talked alone on the roof, catching a breeze off the hills. We sat downstairs, very still, leaning towards the window, listening. As expected, Nicodemus presented his argument like a politician and Torah scholar. The pharisee of pharisees. But Jesus didn't answer as we expected. Blunt. No rhetoric, no room for debate. He matched Nicodemus' brilliance point by point.

"My life is dedicated to following God's law . . ." Nicodemus' words lingered in the night sky aglow from the temple where he began and ended his days. "We obey to the smallest detail. We know something is wrong with our system but we dream God will send us Somebody someday to make it right. Until then, we do our best, hoping for God's approval. Expecting . . . reassurance? I've done all I can and still I wonder what else He requires."

Imagine Jesus answering something like this: *Your best isn't good enough. Sincerity, obedience—they're not enough. Your heritage, not enough. You're an excellent Jew, Nicodemus, but you must be born again.*

All us eavesdroppers sat up straight and looked around. In all our years with the Teacher, we never heard this before. *Born again?* Nicodemus must have been confused, too.

Jesus explained that what we need is life. Life from within. Life from above. Only God can give us the satisfaction we're after. You don't need to twist His arm, He's wants to do this in you. Unless a man is reborn, he is powerless to see God.

Just then, a gust of wind blew across the roof, scattering leaves, knocking over a pot.

"His work in you is like that. Like the wind. Invisible, strong, we see only its result. But it begins when you believe in Him and in return He gives you a new birth."

"But how is this so?" He muttered to himself as much to Jesus.

"You've tried so hard; you're a faithful servant, but God doesn't accept you because you earn it. It's in His gift. He loves you so much that He gave His Son to do the work on your behalf. Believe this and you'll have the whole and lasting life you're after. And not just life here, but life to come."

They talked late into the night. When they said shalom, Nicodemus knew it was not goodbye. I watched the honorable old man turn down the dark street, his steps slow at first, then picking up till by the time he turned the corner towards the temple, he almost ran.

He came looking for a miracle and was surprised when the miracle happened in him.

Tomorrow: *One on one with Jesus who prays for you*

 Let's talk about it:

1. Has there ever been a time in your life when you said, "I've done all I can and still I wonder what else He requires"? Have you ever tried to earn God's gift of life? What changed your thinking?

2. Jesus used the metaphor of the wind for how God works in our lives. How do you relate to this picture? Do you have a story of how God was like the wind in your life?

DAY 10

Bread

The One who feeds us

When Jesus looked up and saw a great crowd coming toward him, he said to Philip, "Where shall we buy bread for these people to eat?" He asked this only to test him, for he already had in mind what he was going to do." John 6:5-6

Maybe I won't have enough . . . We all fear it. Usually it's about money, but it could also be about time or love or some other exhaustible resource. If we let it, these worries eat our lunch.

Today we meet Jesus on a beautiful grass slope on the north end of the Sea of Galilee. It's April A.D. 32, the week before Passover. This time next year Jesus will go to the Cross.

Jesus just got the hard news that John the Baptist had been executed and He was trying to get some space to grieve and be with His disciples. But the crowds show up—wanting more miracles so Jesus turns their arrival into a lesson.

Perhaps with a twinkle in His eye He asked His disciple, Philip, *"Where can we buy bread to feed these people?"* Philip's home was just over the hill in Bethsaida. Perhaps he had connections? (Jesus already knew what He was going to do.)

117

Philip, the meticulous one, now exasperated said, "A year's salary wouldn't be enough to buy bread for each person to get even a bite. We won't ever have enough."

And with that Jesus tells the disciples to invite everyone to have a seat at His table. He took the tiny lunch offered by a boy—and made it enough for five thousand hungry men and their families. The satisfied people all said it reminded them of the Passover story and how God fed them with manna, enough for each day for forty years.

When the meal was over, the disciples, gathered what was left—twelve baskets, enough for each one of them (in keeping with tradition that servants could enjoy the leftovers.) Imagine Philip, now with hands full, looking at Jesus.

"I am the Bread of Life." Jesus said. "Come to Me and you'll never be hungry again."

So why is it that we trust God to give us eternal life, but not our daily bread? Like Philip, we worry what we have is never enough.

Take a seat at God's table and let Him fill you again. When you're fearful of not having enough:

1. Ask Him: what lesson are You teaching me in this hunger? Ask yourself: am I willing to receive what He gives and lack what He withholds?

2. Don't hoard or withhold out of fear. Remember the twelve baskets *left over*. This is not a lesson to how to get along with less or how to live more simply. It's the opposite—ask the Lord to show you how to live more abundantly in Christ. How to go deeper. How to press on to all God has for you.

3. Welcome the opportunity to grow. Say, "Stretch my faith, Lord!" Say no to the voices that push you with "wants" and "needs" and instead say 'yes' to what God wants to give you in this unique season. You don't need anything He has not provided. This is the contented life.

We get hungry for more than food and thirsty for more than drink. Our souls need something that neither the world nor each other can satisfy. Only in God is our soul at rest. Only He offers the food that satisfies—the Bread of Life offers you Himself.

Jesus invites you to His table, *Come empty; leave full.*

Tomorrow: *One on one with Jesus, the One we hope for*

 Let's talk about it:

1. "So why is it that we trust God to give us eternal life, but not our daily bread?" Do you identify with this question?
2. Re-read the three questions above. Which one speaks directly to your heart?

DAY 11

Convinced
The One we hope for

Getting into one of the boats, which was Simon's, he asked him to put out a little from the land. And he sat down and taught the people from the boat. And when he had finished speaking, he said to Simon, "Put out into the deep and let down your nets for a catch." And Simon answered, "Master, we toiled all night and took nothing! But at your word I will let down the nets." And when they had done this, they enclosed a large number of fish, and their nets were breaking. Luke 5:3-6

Imagine this interview with Jesus' disciples: *Describe the moment you knew He was Messiah*—the One to give your whole life to.

Peter Luke 5:1-11

Early on I knew He was something important, I just didn't know what. Once we fished all night but caught nothing. That was the day Jesus taught on the shore near our boats and the people crowded Him out, so He came over and asked me to take Him out in a skiff so He could teach from the water. So I did.

When He was done teaching, He said, "let's go fish." And I, the experienced one, wanted to say, "It's a bad day for fish, plus it's mid-day—you don't fish mid-day." But the look in His eyes made me say, "Sure, whatever you want."

We went to a deep eddy and I threw out the net. I glanced at Him and He was grinning. A full white smile under His dark, bushy beard. *What?* And then the net yanked so strong I almost went in. *Fish!* I'd never seen so many fish. He laughed so hard He almost went in! And the skiff filled up with flipping, silvery fins and we were taking on water and still He laughed.

Later onshore, with a hand on my shoulder, He said just as sure as He told me my name, He said, "From now on you will catch men." And that's the day I anchored my boat, left my nets, and followed Him.

Andrew John 1:35-44

I think I knew the first time I saw Him teach. I had been following the prophet-preacher John, who was baptizing in the Jordan. One day John pointed to Jesus walking towards us and said, "Look— it's God's Passover Lamb! He forgives the sins of the world! This is who I've been talking about!"

I didn't waste time but started after Jesus. *Is what John said true?* Jesus turned and asked, "What do you want?" not in a rude way, but more inviting. But how could I say, *Are You Him? Is it true? Did God send You?* Instead, my friend and I asked Him where He was staying. We wanted more than a roadside chat. He took us to His friends' house and we sat at their table and Jesus talked and talked and opened up the prophets and the law for us. With it, He opened our hearts and mine beat so hard in my chest that I could hear it say, *It's Him, It's Him, It's Him.* He is the Promised One.

The first person I had to tell was my brother. *We found Him,* I told Peter. *We found the Messiah.*

Nathanael John 1:45-51

It was like that for me, too; I knew the first day. Philip told me they had found the Messiah—but he said He was from Nazareth. I sniped how could anything good come from that backwater town? I was a rabbinic student, perhaps with a head a little too big for my yarmulke. But I was sincere in my longing for Messiah.

Just that morning I had prayed for Israel's redemption as I sat under the fig tree. It is our custom to pray for the Redeemer to come while sitting under the branches of our national symbol. My teachers say, "he who, when he prays, does not pray for the coming of the Messiah, has not prayed at all." My classmates and I debated about Messiah's coming; we believed it would be in our generation. So, later that day when I met Jesus and He said, "I saw you under the fig tree," I thought, *who else could have heard my prayer for the Messiah then the Messiah Himself?*" I dropped to my knees and worshipped Him then and there and every day since. Oy, was I wrong about Nazareth!

Tomorrow: *One on one with Jesus on the water*

 Let's talk about it:

1. When did you first know Jesus was the Savior? Did you know right away or was it a long process of discovery?
2. Ask your friends who walk with the Lord to share with you how they first came to Jesus.

DAY 12

Fear

with the One who calls you out of the boat

But when the disciples saw him walking on the sea, they were terrified, and said, "It is a ghost!" and they cried out in fear. But immediately Jesus spoke to them, saying, "Take heart; it is I. Do not be afraid." And Peter answered him, "Lord, if it is you, command me to come to you on the water." He said, "Come." So Peter got out of the boat and walked on the water and came to Jesus. But when he saw the wind, he was afraid, and beginning to sink he cried out, "Lord, save me." Jesus immediately reached out his hand and took hold of him, saying to him, "O you of little faith, why did you doubt?" Matthew 14:26-31

Yes, it's irrational but that doesn't make it less frightening.

Once I was a fisherman who was scared of the water; there, I said it. I lived my whole life around water and still it hid a mystery that left me in a cold sweat.

Andrew and I grew up with our dad's stories of the deep. "Be careful when the water is calm, Simon, because that's when you are passing over the abyss." Another night he'd say, "Be careful when waves are high, Andrew; it's a sign that in the deep, Baal is battling the gods." When storms dropped over the mountain at a moment's notice, you could easily be caught in the depths with who knows what happening beneath you.

Like on that night. After Rabbi fed the crowds at Bethsaida with a boy's lunch, the sun was setting and Jesus sent us ahead to Gennesaret. He wanted to pray, He said. We'd meet Him over there in an hour or two.

But with the darkness came a storm that drove us to the depths. Each swell took us closer, we thought, to Baal's battle below. Then Andrew and the others screamed, "Look . . . a ghost!"

And there He was. Not a ghost, but our Rabbi, walking on the water like He was taking a Sabbath stroll. "Courage, my boys! It's Me. Don't be afraid."

For the first time, I listened to Him rather than my fear. I said, *If it's You, then let me come to you.* And He waved me in, *C'mon.* So, I got out of the boat and stood on a wave. Only when I looked down did I sink. *Lord, save me!* And He did. With laughing eyes, He said, *"I have you . . . why do you doubt?"*

That night, He put my fears of the deep to rest. He convinced me His power was greater than any evil. Now when I'm on the water at night, I remember Him strolling by. When fear grips me I remember, *"I have you . . . why do you doubt?"*

Sometimes God uses the deep to teach us something deep.

Fear reminds us of our human-ness, of how much we need God. But how do you reach out to Him when you're afraid?

"You humble yourself in God's hand," a more seasoned Simon Peter wrote years later. "Give yourself and your fears to Him." Always the fisherman, he said it like this, "Cast your anxieties on Him (cast—like throwing a net)." Because He loves you. Because He's got the power to save you from sinking. Because He's got you.

Tomorrow: *One on one with Jesus and a desperate dad.*

 Let's talk about it:

1. "Fear reminds us of how much we need God." Agree/
    Disagree. Why?
2. How do you "throw your nets" on God when you're anxious
    or afraid?

DAY 13

Traffic

with the One who is always on time

Then came one of the rulers of the synagogue, Jairus by name, and seeing him, he fell at his feet and implored him earnestly, saying, "My little daughter is at the point of death. Come and lay your hands on her, so that she may be made well and live." And he went with him. And a great crowd followed him and thronged about him. Mark 5:22-24

At times, waiting for an answer from God feels like driving an ambulance through heavy traffic. Turn the siren louder if you want, but no one's moving. You can't get through. You're in a hurry but God is not.

It must have felt like that to Jairus, the leader from the synagogue who searched out Jesus when his sick daughter took a turn for the worse.

Jesus can help. He restored blind men and the lame. He delivered the boy with a demon. He can save my sweet lamb. I must get Jesus to her and fast!

When Jairus asked Him, Jesus agreed to come. But right when they pushed through the foot traffic in Capernaum, something stopped Him. *No, no, let's go, let's go. Don't you understand my daughter is dying?*

But Jesus didn't sense the urgency. He paused, turned, and asked the ridiculous question to the crowd, "Who touched me?" Jairus almost picked Jesus up to carry Him home.

Then Jairus spotted his servant in the crowd, and hope drained away. The servant confirmed it: She's dead. Urgency over. They were too late.

Then why in the world would Jesus say, *"No fear, Jairus, only believe"?* Believe what? She's gone. Nevertheless, Jesus pressed on. He cut through the crowd and through the wail of mourners at Jairus's house and went right to where Jairus' daughter lay dead.

She was already gray. Her spirit—gone. Her whimsy—gone. The twelve-year-old who danced and giggled—*gone.* That is, until Jesus took her limp hand. He leaned in and whispered, *"Talitha kum!"* Aramaic for *"Little lamb, stand up!"*

And life flickered behind her eyelids and a rosy warmth filled her cheeks. Then the little sleeping beauty woke up!

That day Jairus learned a mysterious lesson about God's timing and purposes: they're not the same as ours. That was then. What about now?

What about the day we plead with God for help, and all we get is silence? If you've not done that yet, you will. The one who follows God by faith is always asked to wait. And at least as important as what you wait for, is the work God wants to do in you while you wait. This side of heaven we won't know what God is up to but no doubt, God is at work, writing a story of such beauty and symmetry our minds can't receive it now.

The view of life in front of us is only half the story.

If you're waiting, continue to pray. Continue to believe. And in the meantime, be certain God is not only better than your fears, He's also better than your hopes.

Tomorrow: *One on one with Jesus and the woman with cancer*

 Let's talk about it:

1. If you're waiting on God for an answer that feels urgent, what about this story encourages you? What are you learning?
2. "The view of life in front of us is only half the story." What do you think this means?

DAY 14

Wings

The One who heals

Jesus said, "Someone touched me, for I perceive that power has gone out from me." And when the woman saw that she was not hidden, she came trembling, and falling down before him declared in the presence of all the people why she had touched him, and how she had been immediately healed. And he said to her, "Daughter, your faith has made you well; go in peace." Luke 8:46-48

Yesterday, we watched Jesus stop in a crowd and ask, "Who touched me?" Today we meet the one who interrupted.

Let's call her Susan. Susan has some kind of incurable cancer and is willing to do anything to feel better again. What should last five days each month for her had flowed for more than 4,380 days straight. She saw one doctor after the next—and not one of them helped her. In fact, a few hurt her. All of them left her drained and broke.

What hurt Susan most was the ugly label, "unclean." Her husband couldn't touch her, she couldn't go to temple, or light the

Sabbat evening candles. She couldn't eat the Passover meal, or any meal, with her family. She lingered, unwelcomed, on the fringes of her former life. Exhausted, humiliated, sick, and alone.

Not surprising, news of a Healer spread quickly in the hopeless community of the unclean. When Susan heard about this Jesus, some little bit of hope stirred faith in her. *If she could just get close enough to touch Him...she'd hide in the crowd. No one would see.*

So, with the courage only the desperate know, Susan made her move. As Jesus walked by, she reached out and touched His prayer shawl and just the fringes.

Immediately her body flooded with colorful, electric life. The Healer whirled around, "Who touched Me?" And that's where we pick up the story.

His tone was more surprise than accusation. *His* power met *her* faith and something left His body. *Whoa!* He searched the crowd— and when their eyes met, He smiled. What audacity! Far from superstition, He saw a confidence in Him that cured her. *"Daughter, your faith has made you well; go in peace."*

Did you hear that? He called her *daughter.* It had been a lifetime since anyone spoke to her so tenderly. And He wished her *shalom.* Peace—that *wholeness* of life from being in right relationship with God. For the first time in twelve years—no, in her life—Susan stood whole and clean.

Malachi 4:2 prophesied that the Messiah would come with "healing in his wings." The Hebrew word for "wings," *kanaph,* is also the word for "borders" describing the long tassels on the corners of a Jewish prayer shawl. The Messiah was prophesied to have healing in His tassels. Susan probably didn't know this, she simply grasped at the last threads of hope as the Savior walked by.

Tomorrow: *One on one with Jesus, the storyteller*

Let's talk about it:

1. What do you need to be healed from? What is Jesus doing in your life in the process?

2. "Peace—that *wholeness* of life from being in right relationship with God." Have you ever experienced people like this? Describe how it feels; what is it like?

DAY 15

Stories
The One who knows your story

But blessed are your eyes, for they see, and your ears, for they hear. For truly, I say to you, many prophets and righteous people longed to see what you see, and did not see it, and to hear what you hear, and did not hear it.
Matthew 13 3:16-17

Jesus helped people connect with God in a way they weren't used to. Usually religious talk is so filled with complicated rhetoric and theological terms that, to be honest, we look the other way. Life is complicated enough, you know?

But Jesus taught, formally and in every day chats, by telling stories—unremarkable happenings that usually make us smile . . . then pause, and then later laugh out loud when we realize the little "truth-bomb" He set off in our hearts. The next day when we're *still* thinking about the story, we realize He taught us theology after all.

"Parables," those common, little stories in the Gospels, literally means "thrown alongside something," just the way Jesus threw these stories in conversation. They're about the things we talk and text about—work, friends, family, about what happens on trips, about how our gardens grow. Jesus' stories don't usually tell us something new, but they get us to notice what's been there all along. Like a magnifying glass, they focus our attention on something God is up to.

Using a story to convey what life in God looks like is a tricky way to speak about holy things. But when you can connect all that you know and don't know about yourself to all that you know and don't know about God, it works. Sometimes the lesson speaks for itself, sometimes Jesus explains it. Sometimes the lessons are only clear to those open to learn about real life in God.

Parables are a slow drip into your soul that convinces you God really is engaged with you today—in your trip to Walmart and walking the dog and that hard thing between you and your sister. In His parables, Jesus confirms our far-off hope that He is moving closer, taking us somewhere in our hearts.

So when you think about Jesus' parables and read them for yourself (there's more than forty in Luke), picture your own stories when you discover what life in God is like. Ask God to show you what He's working on in your life.

Because, as Jesus taught us, He's just as proud of the artful way He's writing your story as He is proud of the birds on your window sill and the Great Coral Reef and the way the stars spin through space. God's behind every one of them.

Tomorrow*: One on one with Jesus, who gives your life back*

 Let's talk about it:

1. What's one of your favorite parables from the Bible? Why do you like it?
2. Share with someone today one of your stories that shows how God is working in your life.

DAY 16

Home again
The One who gives life back

While he was in one of the cities, there came a man full of leprosy. And when he saw Jesus, he fell on his face and begged him, "Lord, if you will, you can make me clean." And Jesus stretched out his hand and touched him, saying, "I will; be clean." And immediately the leprosy left him.
Luke 5:12-13

Everyone suffers, I know that. Most everyone heals too, though perhaps scarred. But when my gravest fears came true, I knew I wouldn't recover.

Leprosy takes you to your grave inch by inch. First your skin dies, then nerves die. Your good life rots away. You're still you, but no one can see you behind the gore.

Leprosy robs you of feeling till eventually your heart stops, perhaps years before it actually does. You can't feel love, because you're not loved anymore. You don't remember gratitude, because you have nothing left to be thankful for.

My family held my funeral, and I watched from a distance. I was dead to them. My wife screamed my name, "Simon, Simon, my love" and I couldn't even cry.

Hope is a dangerous thing. When the Healer came to Bethany, I didn't go to the square where others crowded Him. But later that day, Jesus came looking for me. He invited my poor, unclean stump of a hand to touch His. "Do you want to be healed, Simon?"

Of course, the miracle He did in a moment restored life to my body but it's the miracle He did in my heart that won't stop these tears from coming, even now.

I sit across from Him at my family's table. I said, "You always have a place in my home, Jesus," and to my surprise, He came.

To my home, to my table, to my heart. My wife, smiling again, calls us to a feast. My grandson on my knee. I look now across the happy uproar of plates passing and wine pouring and music playing and favor flowing—to meet the eyes of my Healer looking back at me. What do I see in His eyes? *Love, pure love.*

He came to give you and me this glad kind of love. He stared death in the face to give us this glad kind of eternal life. Someday when sin and sickness are gone forever, you and I will sit around the table like this again, together and with Him.

I once was dead, and now I'm alive for the first time—body, spirit, and soul. All because He came looking for me.

Only when my grandson reached up to grab my chin did my gaze break from His and the music filled my ears again. Now Jesus laughs with my children, tears glistening in His eyes as we break bread.

"Trust Him sooner," that's what I'd say to you today in your pain. It took this miracle mystery to give me this life today, oh, I wish I would have believed Him sooner. And you? Say with me, too, "make my heart your home, Lord Jesus."

Tomorrow: *One on one with Jesus who satisfies.*

Let's talk about it:

1. Do you realize just how much Jesus loves you? None of us really grasp how deep and wide is the love of God for us. Read Romans 8:38-39.

2. Look up John 15:1-11. Every time you read the word "abide," substitute the phrase, "be at home with." Imagine just how much Jesus wants to be at home with you!

DAY 17

Thirsty

The One who satisfies

On the last day of the feast, the great day, Jesus stood up and cried out, "If anyone thirsts, let him come to me and drink. Whoever believes in me, as the Scripture has said, 'Out of his heart will flow rivers of living water.'" John 7:37-46

You have to wonder if He just couldn't keep quiet any longer.

There He was, smack dab in the middle of Temple Mount, crowded with thousands of people—soldiers, lawyers, and angry priests scheming to trap and kill Him—and Jesus stands up and shouts.

"Here, over here," it's like He said. "It's Me you're looking for!"

It was September 17, A.D. 32. Rarely do we know a specific date from Jesus' life, but history tells us this was the date for Feast of Tabernacles that year. Israel's celebration, Sukkoth as it's known today, remembers how God provided for Israel as they wandered the wilderness. It's a week-long Thanksgiving holiday with all the family and feasting like we enjoy.

Israel has two seasons, wet and dry. A big part of Sukkoth was asking God for rain for the next year. If they didn't get rain in the spring and fall, they didn't eat the next year. On this last day of the holiday, crowds packed the temple to chant prayers. ("As You provided water in the wilderness, send us rain or else we'll die!")

Behind all the ceremony, Jesus heard the people ask God for more than rain. He was a Savior, after all—come to seek and rescue those who needed saving. He likely sat there in the court hidden in plain sight from His enemies, and just couldn't stay quiet. He stood up and shouted something like, "Hey, everyone! Are you thirsty? Come to Me! Believe in Me, and out of your heart will flow rivers of living water!"

You can imagine the stir. Some whispered, "That sounds like the Messiah!" Others shook their heads, "No, I knew him as a boy in Galilee." And later when the officers were asked by the aggravated chief priests and Pharisees, "Why didn't you bring him in?" the officers shrugged their shoulders, "No one ever spoke like this man!"

It's true. No one else ever said, "I am everything you're looking for." "I am your rain in the wilderness." "I am your Sukkoth." No one else ever invited the thirsty to, "Come to Me and I will satisfy you with Living Water." No one else ever qualified to be their Savior.

But He did. And on that September afternoon, Jesus invited to Himself everyone who would come. Many came. More believe and follow Him today all the way Home.

Tomorrow: *One on one with Jesus on the mountain side*

 Let's talk about it:

1. Have you ever prayed for rain? Or for provision from God? How did it make you feel?
2. Are you satisfied by your relationship with God? Why/ why not?

DAY 18

Blessed

The One who hints at heaven

Seeing the crowds, he went up on the mountain, and when he sat down, his disciples came to him. And he opened his mouth and taught them, saying: "Blessed are the poor in spirit, for theirs is the kingdom of heaven. . ."
Matthew 5:1-3

We all have things working against us when it comes to believing God. It was no different that day for the people who sat on the hillside overlooking the lake. They'd come to listen to the Teacher. He who was "the Word become flesh" had a way with words—drawing or repelling hearts like a magnet.

Jesus' ideas run upside down to what most people consider important. He confirms our suspicions that life is not what it should be nor what it will be. The "Sermon on the Mount" could easily be called, "What it will be like in heaven" because He describes what we look like when God's will is done in us.

Picture Jesus standing there with His back to the Sea of Galilee and a sea of faces in front of Him, leaning in.

"Blessed are you;" He says, picking out the faces who believed He would come; faces He had in mind when He left heaven for the Cross.

"Blessed are you . . ." Listen closely to who Jesus is calling. They're not spiritual superheroes. They know they don't have it all together but keep coming back for more of God. They're the humble. The ones, though not perfect, know someday they will be. The ones with undivided hearts for Him.

This is just a glimpse of God's kingdom on earth and what it looks like if we lived as if it was true—like Jesus did. Let it serve as a prayer for His will to be done in you.

Blessed are you, poor in spirit . . . *I am gentle and humble in heart* . . . Matt.11:29

LORD, CREATE THIS HEART IN ME.

Blessed are you when you are meek. . . *He was led like a lamb to the slaughter Isaiah 53:7*

LORD, CREATE THIS HEART IN ME.

Blessed are the merciful . . . *Father, forgive them. Luke 23:34*

LORD, CREATE THIS HEART IN ME.

Blessed are the peacemakers . . . *For He Himself is our peace* . . . *Ephesians 2:14*

LORD, CREATE THIS HEART IN ME.

Blessed are you when people insult you . . . *They said, 'He saved others; let Him save Himself Luke 23:35*

LORD, CREATE THIS HEART IN ME.

You are the light of the world . . . . *Jesus said, "I am the light of the world. Whoever follows me will never walk in darkness, but will have the light of life." John 8:12*

LORD, CREATE THIS HEART IN ME.

Eight blessings start as a window and become a mirror of God in the person of Jesus. He came to show us how it's done and to invite us to join Him in the reality He's creating.

Jesus said life on this side of heaven is hard, but oh, so much more rich if we choose to live as if we're already there.

Tomorrow: *One on one with Jesus and an accused woman*

 Let's talk about it:

1. Which of Jesus' eight "beatitudes" speaks to you?
2. What does the prayer, "Lord, create this heart in me," mean to you?

DAY 19

Accused

The One who dispels the darkness

"Let him who is without sin among you be the first to throw a stone at her." And once more he bent down and wrote on the ground. But when they heard it, they went away one by one, beginning with the older ones, and Jesus was left alone with the woman standing before him.
John 8:7-9

Clearly, it was less about the woman caught in adultery and more about trapping Jesus.

A "religious" mob of men threw a barely dressed woman in front of Jesus one morning while He was teaching. "Teacher, this woman bedded a man who isn't her husband. In the Law, Moses says to stone her. What do you say?"

Jesus saw right through them. They accused her so they could accuse Him. They picked up rocks, ready to throw them (at her? At Him? Either would be fine.) If they could just catch Him breaking either Roman law or Moses' law . . . their righteous indignation would be satisfied. More than justice executed on her, they wanted Him.

Jesus answered their unanswerable question by bending down and writing something in the dirt with His finger. The shouting stopped and the dust settled. Jesus then straightened up and looked around, "The sinless one goes first: go ahead, throw your stone."

Their eyes shifted from Jesus to the words. Feet shuffled. Eyes dropped. Silence. Then the thud of rocks hitting the dirt and footsteps scurrying away. Though they came as one, they left one by one.

We're not told what Jesus wrote in the dirt. Maybe it was a list of names from the crowd who were also guilty of adultery. Maybe it was a list of sins—secret sins—and every accuser saw theirs plain as day.

That's the funny thing about sin. It sneaks up on you. You think it's private—but secret sin on earth is open scandal in heaven. Nothing is hidden from God.

Not until Jesus and the woman stood there alone did He turn His attention to her. We don't even know her name, but Jesus does. He knows the name of her lover, too, and all about the betrayal and the lies that brought her to this dark place.

Jesus told her to look up. "Does anyone condemn you? . . . then neither do I."

Jesus isn't going soft on adultery; He's giving her a chance to repent. "Go and sin no more."

Perhaps that was the first mercy she'd ever been shown. And for the first time, the darkness in her life began to lift.

Funny, too, that in the very next verse, John tells us, *Jesus spoke to them, saying, 'I am the light of the world. Whoever follows me will not walk in darkness but will have the light of life.'*

Tomorrow: *One on one with Jesus at the well*

Let's talk about it:

1. Before pointing out someone else's sin, imagine what Jesus could write in the dirt about your sins . . . Have you asked Him to forgive you?
2. Do you remember how dark your world was before Jesus forgave you? Perhaps it's still dark. Be quiet for a moment and remember. Now, thank Him for rescuing you when no one else can.

DAY 20

Loved

with the One who meets you

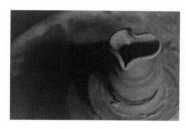

So the woman left her water jar and went away into town and said to the people, "Come, see a man who told me all that I ever did. Can this be the Christ?" They went out of the town and were coming to him.
John 4:28-30

Everyone longs to be loved by somebody—to be someone's "person." To many, this desperate search has cost them a world of hurt, compromise, and loss. Too easily, we transfer this rejection to our relationship with God.

If you've ever wondered if God could *really* love you, then meet Jesus at the well.

At Jacob's Well that day in Samaria, Jesus planned a special date with, let's call her Abby. He wanted a private conversation so He sent His men into town to get lunch. Jesus waited for her alone.

No one goes to the well in the heat of the day. We can assume Abby is either living on the bad side of a moral decision or she was deeply depressed. Maybe she couldn't deal with the other women's chit-chat. Whatever the reason, Abby was hurting and hiding in the margins.

145

She must have thought Jesus crazy for asking *her* for a drink—a *Samaritan* (a racial issue) and a *woman* (a social issue). They both knew she was the one dying of thirst.

She wasn't dumb, after all. She recognized His claim right away. "Anyone who drinks the water I give will never thirst—not ever." *Messiah? Could it be?*

That's when Jesus told her everything she had done in her search for love. Painful, private things. *How do You know that?* He must have answered her without any shame in His voice because for the first time, she looked up and met love. The real thing.

She gave Him water . . . He offered her Himself.

Jesus knows your soul only feels complete when you're satisfied in Him. Only then can you find real intimacy across the dinner table or lying beside you in bed—a closeness that pictures your relationship with Him.

Too often we think we only can be loved if we measure up. A woman measures her worth by the way her body curves or doesn't curve. A man, by how he ranks at work, by the money he makes, or by how tall or muscular he stands.

But Jesus offers you His love based on what you can choose. You can choose to believe Him. You can choose to humble yourself under His choices for your life. You can choose to be saved and safe and loved. You can choose life—fulfilled, beautiful life—by standing next to Jesus.

That's what Abby did that day. By faith she knew she needed what He held out. She knew she needed rescue. Her story not only quenched her thirst for living water, it convinced the whole town to follow Jesus, the Messiah.

Tomorrow: *One on one with Jesus and the demons*

Let's talk about it:

1. Does it comfort you—or make you uncomfortable—that Jesus knows every detail of your story? Why?

2. How did you feel the day that you realized that you needed saving? Did you reach out to Jesus right away or did it take a while?

DAY 21

Set Free

with the One who rescues us from darkness

In the synagogue there was a man who had the spirit of an unclean demon, and he cried out with a loud voice, "Ha! What have you to do with us, Jesus of Nazareth? Have you come to destroy us? I know who you are—the Holy One of God." But Jesus rebuked him, saying, "Be silent and come out of him!" Luke 4:33-35

There's another story, older than earth, happening alongside our current story. About the time Jesus arrived to preach about eternal life, a sinister, spiritual battle with Satan and his demons exploded on the scene, especially in the Galilee.

God originally created demons as holy angels. Their home was heaven where they served and worshiped God. At some point in eternity past, pride fueled their rebellion against God, along with their leader, Lucifer/Satan. As punishment, Jesus threw Satan and millions of demons (one third of the heavenly host) out of heaven and prepared an eternal place of agony, "the lake of fire," for them. They know their fate. And they know they're working against time.

It happened on a day when Jesus was preaching in the synagogue at Capernaum. A local crowd packed the place as He read Isaiah 61 and announced, "I am here to rescue the spiritual prisoners held by the devil and to destroy his works."

Then from the crowd, a man possessed by a demon screamed out in terror.

'We know who you are, Jesus of Nazareth! You're the Holy One of God. Are You here to destroy us? Is this the time? Is it now? Have You come to send us to the lake of fire?'

Jesus pointed right at him: "You shut up and get out of him!" And the demon shook the man down in front of them . . . and left him. With just a word from across the room, Jesus overpowered the demon. (If Jesus threw Satan out of heaven, He could throw a demon out of a man.) He can also deliver us from sin and death and Satan and hell.

That's how powerful Jesus is. His good news shatters the stranglehold Satan has on people; it smashes prison walls. His good news breaks the chains sin wraps around us. It frees every sinner who calls out His name. That is the power of our Lord Jesus Christ.

As Jesus traveled around Galilee, people begged Him to rescue them from demonic control. The war with evil was on and Jesus proved Himself the victor again and again. We only know a few accounts, but it happened all the time.

The same is true today. Demons know who Jesus is, and it makes them shudder. They read the Bible. They know the end of the story. It terrifies them to know their time is short, so they work their subtle craft to keep as many imprisoned to sin and death as they can.

If Jesus is your Savior, then God has "delivered you from the domain of darkness and transferred you to the kingdom of His beloved Son." You have nothing to fear from the spiritual darkness. Strengthen your confidence in Jesus by filling your mind with God's Word about Satan's strategies and your victory in Christ. Equip yourself with a shield of faith and the sword of truth:

John 16:33   Romans 8:37-39
2 Corinthians 10:4-5   Ephesians 6:10-11
Colossians 1:13-14   2 Thessalonians 3:3

Tomorrow: *One on one with Jesus and a mom who wouldn't quit*

 Let's talk about it:

1. Review the facts about satanic warfare here. What truth do
   you want to remember when you feel caught or discouraged
   by this spiritual battle?
2. Read over the verses listed. Pick one to memorize so you'll
   have it ready next time you need it.

DAY 22

Crumbs

with the One who answers faith

But immediately a woman whose little daughter had an unclean spirit heard of him and came and fell down at his feet. Now the woman was a Gentile, a Syrophoenician by birth. And she begged him to cast the demon out of her daughter. And he said to her, "Let the children be fed first, for it is not right to take the children's bread and throw it to the dogs." But she answered him, "Yes, Lord; yet even the dogs under the table eat the children's crumbs." Mark 7:25-28

Nothing takes us to our knees faster than a sick child. We'll trade our dignity, we'll beg, we'll bargain—we'll do anything to get relief for our little one.

It happened on a day when Jesus was trying to get away from the crowds for some needed relief. He took the disciples forty miles north into Gentile country. Hopefully no one would know them there. But there was a woman, just one, who recognized Jesus. In spite of the fact she was a Greek, a Phoenician from Syria, she believed Jesus could heal her daughter. And she didn't mind asking Him to do so, again and again.

"Please, sir, please, sir, please, help me. My daughter is cruelly terrorized by a demon. Only You can help us, Master." She followed Jesus around, begging Him. She wouldn't quit.

"Send this woman away, Lord. She's driving us crazy!" the disciples pleaded. But Jesus didn't say a word to either of them. Nothing made this mother walk away, not when hope was so close. She wasn't going home to her scarred, terrorized daughter without relief.

Home: just imagine what a wreck it was. They hadn't known peace since that demon moved in. So, this gutsy mom paid no attention to the long list why she didn't qualify for help from the Lord—and instead kept asking, "Please, sir, please help me."

Finally, He answered her—but it wasn't what anyone expected. *"It's not right to take bread out of children's mouths and throw it to dogs."*

What did Jesus say? This rude remark wasn't like Him. But Jesus knew exactly what He was doing. He was fishing for faith.

Her come-back was quick. Humbly, and perhaps with a twinkle in her eye she threw Jesus' words back to Him, "You're right, Master, but even the puppies feed on crumbs from the table."

Even if I'm not entitled to sit as a guest at the Jewish Messiah's table, at least I can ask for a crumb of God's mercy...That would be enough, she seemed to say. *Just a crumb of grace.*

Can't you just picture Jesus' smile at her charming challenge? She passed the test and He agreed. *"Oh, woman, your faith is beautiful. What you want is what you get!"*

And that was enough for her. She shut up and went home (by faith) and found her daughter at peace, lying in bed. The demon was gone.

In a land Jews despised, Jesus surprised everyone—a desperate woman who risked trusting a Jewish rabbi and a bunch of confused disciples who learned God will save anyone who calls out His name in faith.

Tomorrow: *One on one with Jesus and the generous pauper*

 Let's talk about it:

1. Can you relate to this mom pleading for her child?
2. Have you ever, or are you now, praying for something that only God can provide? If in the past, what truth/lesson can you share?
3. Have you ever thought that some people are out of reach of God's grace?

DAY 23

All

The One who sees your heart

He called his disciples to him and said to them, "Truly, I say to you, this poor widow has put in more than all those who are contributing to the offering box. ⁴⁴ For they all contributed out of their abundance, but she out of her poverty has put in everything she had, all she had to live on." Mark 12:43-44

We are never more like God than when we give. Scripture says where you invest your treasure is where you most want to be.

Some of the poorest people you ever meet give the most to the Lord. Some of the richest people are tight-fisted. How much you have has little impact on your generosity.

Jesus had this on His mind the day He and His disciples sat people-watching in the temple. They hung out near the offering boxes, made of metal and shaped like trumpets. When the wealthy dumped in their money bags, everyone turned at the noise and noticed them.

No one but Jesus noticed the old woman slip by, by the looks of her, a poor widow. The two thin copper coins she dropped into the offering box didn't make a sound. These coins, nicknamed "mites"—meaning "crumbs," were worth next to nothing. They could perhaps buy a handful of flour.

"This poor widow gave more to the collection than all the others put together," Jesus told His men. *"All the others gave what they'll never miss; she gave what she couldn't afford—she gave her all."*

Widows were a vulnerable group in Israel society. Their lives were defined by what they lacked. They had no inheritance rights and little opportunity to make a living. Their survival depended on the mercy of their children or the community.

God's heart is tender toward women who are alone, which explains Jesus' warm spot for widows—maybe because His mother was one. He noticed this widow put in *two* coins. She could have given one copper and used the other to buy a small meal. Instead, she cheerfully gave both. *God will take care of me. He always has.*

Only love motivates generosity like that. She gladly gave all she had to God. It did her heart good to play a part in what He was doing.

How are you like God in your giving? Ask Him today if you can play a part in something that will bring Him glory—some act of ministry in His name. God doesn't need it; but it'll do your heart good to offer your life to Him.

The widow never noticed the young rabbi and His disciples watching her from across the treasury. But they noticed her. In fact, Jesus still watches the offering box—not to see the people whose gift makes the most noise, but to listen for the beat of their heart.

Tomorrow: *One on one with Jesus and Martha.*

Let's talk about it:

1. How are you like God in your giving? Ask Him today if you can play a part in something that will bring Him glory—some act of ministry in His name. Then give.
2. Is giving tithes and offerings easy or hard for you? How about when finances are stretched? How about when finances are ample?

DAY 24

Priorities

The One who wants your love

Martha welcomed him into her house. And she had a sister called Mary, who sat at the Lord's feet and listened to his teaching. But Martha was distracted with much serving. And she went up to him and said, "Lord, do you not care that my sister has left me to serve alone? Tell her then to help me." Luke 10:38-40

It would surprise you what impresses God. We think it would be sacrifice. Hard work. Service. Results. Yet those things rarely impress Him at all.

It took Martha off guard, too. When she welcomed Jesus into her home for a visit and a meal, He likely had His twelve with Him, plus a few other disciples. Maybe the 72 disciples He had recently sent out on itinerant ministry tours showed up, too.

So, let's give Martha a break. It's hard enough to host the Messiah, much less twenty-five or even 100 hungry extra mouths. Factor in the Middle Eastern culture's commitment to generous hospitality, add Martha's get-it-done personality, and stress is written all over this scene.

When she reached her tipping point, Martha scolded Jesus for not appreciating how hard her task was and for not ordering her sister, Mary, to help. *Don't You care? Can't You see?*

Jesus comes off as rather insensitive, even ungrateful, to what it takes to put a meal together—(could we extend that to what it takes to put together a church service or a small group, too?) Unless of course, He knows something we don't . . .

And He kindly put His finger right on it.

"Martha, Martha," the Lord answered her, "you are worried and upset about many things, but few things are needed—or indeed only one."

He saw her hard work but went to motive instead. Did pride drive her anxiety?

Do you see me over here, Jesus? Do You see how well I'm serving You with this big, important task? Isn't it impressive?

Martha's cry for help was more a humble brag. She learned the hard way how easy it is to fail in our strength rather than in our weakness.

"Mary has chosen what is better, and it will not be taken away from her."

Jesus wasn't saying introverts are better than extroverts. Or reflective personalities are better than active ones. Instead, He reminded her we order our lives by what we love. We make time for what we are passionate about and neglect lesser things. Mary was captivated by Jesus and when she sat at His feet, nothing else mattered.

Yes, working hard for Jesus matters. Bible study matters. Service is so important. But not at the neglect of loving Jesus. Love God more than ministry. Set your priorities, not on serving Him or doing His work, but on loving Him with everything you've got.

Tomorrow: *One on one with Jesus who will give you rest.*

Let's talk about it:

1. Do you enjoy working hard for God? Describe what motivates you.

2. "She learned the hard way how easy it is to fail in our strength rather than in our weakness." Agree or disagree?

DAY 25

Come

The One who is your rest

Come to me, all who labor and are heavy laden, and I will give you rest. Take my yoke upon you, and learn from me, for I am gentle and lowly in heart, and you will find rest for your souls. For my yoke is easy, and my burden is light." Matthew 11:28-30

It could have happened on a hot day in Jerusalem.

Jesus was teaching somewhere on Temple Mount; His disciples hung on every word. A crowd listened in to His unique take on truth they've long heard about, but never really understood. Now they get it.

Out of this mix of people, a toddler breaks loose from his parents. They don't notice their boy has wandered off, heading right for the Teacher. The surprised parents are aghast, "Micah! Come back here!" The disciples rush to shoo the kid away. Jesus calms them both.

"Let him come. Such is the kingdom of heaven." And He lifts Micah onto His knee and continues to teach.

At first, Micah plays with the fringe on Jesus' prayer shawl. Then he leans back on Jesus' chest and in the shade of the tree and the comfort of His voice, Micah falls asleep.

Perhaps Jesus looked down and smiled. *"Thank you, Father, Lord of heaven and earth, that you have hidden Your ways from those who think they know it all and revealed them to little children. Yes, that's the way You like to work."*

And looking up to the crowd He asked the crowd if they were worn out? *Weary of a religion that keeps demanding more and giving less? Come to Me and I'll show you how to really rest.* He gets up and returns the sleeping boy to his father's arms. *Walk with Me and watch how I do it. I won't lay anything too heavy on you. My yoke is easy.*

His offer still stands today. If He commands you to rest; He'll show you how.

What does Jesus' rest look like in your life?

- When you rest from work, you trust God to make up for the time you refrain from producing. You trust Him to provide for you as you choose not to provide for yourself.
- When you rest from worry, you remind yourself your life belongs to God and you live for Him. He will take that anxiety and refresh you instead.
- When you rest from accomplishment, you yield to Him life's lesser things and invite Him to order your days. Only then will your life take the shape it's meant to have.

With God, let all things begin. With God, let all things rest.

Tomorrow: *One on one with Jesus and His other disciples*

Let's talk about it:

1. Which of those three bullets do you most need to rest from? (work, worry, accomplishment)
2. What do you hope would happen if you did rest in God (specifically in that one area?)

DAY 26

Disciples, too
with the One who tears down walls

Soon afterward he went on through cities and villages, proclaiming and bringing the good news of the kingdom of God. And the twelve were with him, and also some women who had been healed of evil spirits and infirmities: Mary, called Magdalene, from whom seven demons had gone out, and Joanna, the wife of Chuza, Herod's household manager, and Susanna, and many others, who provided for them out of their means.
Luke 8:1-3

So who paid for travel, food, and lodging for thirteen men for three years? No one took an offering or asked for support. Jesus got no honorarium for His speaking engagements. Who funded Jesus' ministry?

Surprisingly, many women did. Luke tells us a few of their names—Joanna from Herod's high society and Susanna. Mary, James' mother, and Mary Magdalene, and "many others." Not only did Jesus welcome their support, He welcomed them to walk with

Him. In the day, this was just shy of scandalous and certainly a huge paradigm shift. Most rabbis shooed women away. Pharisees were downright scared of them. At best, most men dismissed women—from conversation, from contribution, from their club.

Instead, Jesus broke down the walls that kept women out.

He applauded Mary of Bethany who sat at His feet and listened to Him teach. *"She chose the better..."* He talked doctrine with Martha and with the Samaritan woman at the well. He noticed the quiet, faithful things women did—even a widow giving crumbs to the Temple offering. He praised Jewish and Gentile women alike for their spiritual grit. He welcomed Mary Magdalene to His ministry team—choosing to greet her first after His resurrection.

Nobody did that for women in first century Israel nor for centuries since.

While the typical disciple around Jesus was called, these women just came. Brave women, all of them, stepped forward to follow. To learn. To serve. The women, perhaps more so than the men, really got who Jesus was. Call it intuition or personal experience, they just knew He was the Christ. Jesus had rescued all of them: some from demonic terror, others from physical illness, all from spiritual darkness.

So, with great tenacity, a handful of courageous, devoted women walked in company with Jesus. Likely, they had their share of funny and touching behind-the-scenes stories to tell. They loved Jesus because He first loved them. They showed up in the places and times when it mattered most—at the cross and at His burial.

They must have meant a great deal to Jesus who blatantly broke culture's rules to help them and welcome them so notoriously. They were women of faith, true disciples, whom He called out of the shadows and into lives of influence and impact. He must have meant the world to them.

Tomorrow: *One on one with Jesus and the rich kid*

Let's talk about it:

1. Do you know women like these who love Jesus and give to Jesus with all their hearts? Name a few.

2. What attributes of their character would you like said of you?

DAY 27

Better

with the One who wants to give you more

"Good Teacher, what must I do to inherit eternal life?" ...Jesus, looking at him, loved him, and said to him, "You lack one thing: go, sell all that you have and give to the poor, and you will have treasure in heaven; and come, follow me." Disheartened by the saying, he went away sorrowful, for he had great possessions.
Mark 10:17, 21-22

He had it all. Almost. He was rich, young, and not a stretch to think he might be good-looking, and the recently elected president of the Young Leaders Club of Israel. But something was missing in his life and he knew it.

"Teacher," he asked Jesus, *"What good thing must I do to get eternal life?"* ... as if he could acquire eternal life like he got everything else. But Jesus saw through the swagger. He knew what to poke. He knew the issue that stood in the way of this young man having a whole-hearted, radical, beautiful life in God. For this rich kid, it was his possessions. (His garage was full, we're told.)

Yours might be a different issue. Jesus knows yours, too.

Ask yourself, what's the thing that stands in the way of experiencing the amazing life Jesus wants to give me? What are you holding onto? Maybe it *is* your stuff. Or your rights. Or some important relationship. Or your fears. Or some other pride point.

Or maybe it's what you don't have. "I would follow the Lord, if . . ." and the conditions follow. "If I don't have to be a missionary in Africa." Or, "if I don't have to act or talk weird like some Christians I know."

You might negotiate for something you think is missing, "I'll follow You, if you give me a husband . . . a child . . . a successful career." "If I can do pursue my own path and follow You too, then I'm all for it."

The rich young ruler was willing to pull out his credit card, but Jesus told him he didn't have enough. *Only I'm enough.*

The funny thing is, if you think demanding your rights or dreams will get you to that amazing life, you (and the rich kid) miss the point. When Jesus says, *"I came to give you life—a rich and satisfying life,"* it might look totally different than you dreamed. But the moment after you breathe your last, you'll be so glad you didn't hold on to anything that kept you from this highest and best and most life with Jesus.

The smartest thing you can do today is ask what competes for that singular place in your life that belongs to Jesus alone. Ask Him to show you.

When you don't know what you want but you know something's missing, let God prove Himself to you to be better. He wants to give you more. He wants to give you Himself. Let everything else go.

Tomorrow: *One on one with Jesus and Zacchaeus*

Let's talk about it:

1. Was there a time in your life that you would have asked, *"What good thing must I do to get eternal life?"* What did you think it was?

2. Ask yourself, *what's the thing that stands in the way of experiencing the amazing life Jesus wants to give me?* What competes for that singular place in your life that belongs to Jesus alone. Ask Him to show you.

═══ DAY 28 ═══

Curious

The One who seeks and saves the lost

"Zacchaeus, hurry and come down, for I must stay at your house today." So he hurried and came down and received him joyfully. And when they saw it, they all grumbled, "He has gone in to be the guest of a man who is a sinner." And Zacchaeus stood and said to the Lord, "Behold, Lord, the half of my goods I give to the poor. And if I have defrauded anyone of anything, I restore it fourfold." And Jesus said to him, "Today salvation has come to this house, since he also is a son of Abraham. For the Son of Man came to seek and to save the lost." Luke 19:1-10

Some people who crossed Jesus' path were not especially religious, nor had some great need they wanted Him to fix. Like Zacchaeus in Jericho, many were just curious.

Who wouldn't be? The first century world is small. The miracles Jesus did were huge. His claims to being Messiah, even bigger.

Zacchaeus was Jericho's least loved citizen. As a Roman IRS agent (a legal crook), he charged Jericho's citizens double the tax and pocketed the difference. Maybe just to complete the persona, we're told Zacchaeus was really short. Picture Danny DeVito.

So on that day in Jericho, news on the street was Jesus of Nazareth was on His way through and for all the reasons people flock to see a celebrity, the crowds gathered. Curious at all the fanfare, Zacchaeus thought he'd get a look for himself at this self-proclaimed Messiah. Too bad the crowd kept him from the front. That's when Zacchaeus climbed a tree.

What would he see? A teacher who says profound things? A lunatic who thinks he's God? A prophet out of history? Zacchaeus prided himself on reading people (so he could rip them off.) He'd see about this Jesus.

Picture the scene: Here comes Jesus. The crowd goes wild. Zacchaeus cranes his neck for a glimpse. Then Jesus turns and looks his way. To everyone's shock, Jesus walks right up to the sycamore tree where Zacchaeus is perched. *Well finally, Zacchaeus is going to get what he's got coming. Give it to him, Jesus! Tell him not to rob us anymore!*

Instead, Jesus leans against the tree and says something like, *Hey Zacchaeus, c'mon down here. I want to spend the day with you.*

Without even thinking about how Jesus knew his name, Zacchaeus was stunned by the honor. His flight out of the branches— pure comedy.

The townspeople watched the curious scene of Jesus walking away with Zacchaeus, His arm resting on the short man's shoulders. They'd have given anything to know what the two talked about all day. For years after, the town remembered how later that day Zacchaeus turned over half his bank account to the poor and paid back, four to one, all the cash he'd extorted from them.

They never elected him mayor or anything, but on that day Zacchaeus captured the heart of the town. It all goes back to what Jesus said when they emerged from Zacchaeus' house. *"Today is salvation day in this home!"* He should know since His mission was to "seek and save the lost" and no one was more lost than Zacchaeus. And no one could save better than Jesus.

If it happened here in Jericho, then you can be sure it's happening in your town, too. The least likely person repents and turns to Jesus. How about it?—is it you?

Tomorrow: *One on one with Jesus and the shepherd*

 Let's talk about it:

1. Who do you know that is just curious about Jesus?
2. If they asked you, what would you say to them about Jesus?

DAY 29

Shepherd, Part 2
The One who lays down His life

"Truly, truly, I say to you, he who does not enter the sheepfold by the door but climbs in by another way, that man is a thief and a robber. But he who enters by the door is the shepherd of the sheep. To him the gatekeeper opens. The sheep hear his voice, and he calls his own sheep by name and leads them out. When he has brought out all his own, he goes before them, and the sheep follow him, for they know his voice.
John 10:1-4

The night the spirits told us shepherds where to find the Messiah has stayed with me for 30 years. The memory has nipped at my heels like a sheep dog.

Since then, I've listened to talk of Messiah in Jerusalem. Plenty of imposters come and go; nobody survives the scrutiny. As the years passed and still no Messiah, I doubt what I saw and heard.

It was Matthias, my grandson, who told me about the rabbi from Nazareth. *Nazareth?—well, that can't be Him*, I thought.

"He's doing miracles, Sabba. Isn't it written the Messiah you saw will do miracles? Can we go to Jerusalem? Can we see Him?"

Yes, I was twelve once, too. Sure, we can go to Jerusalem. I have business there, I told my wife. It would be worth the trip to see a miracle-working rabbi.

And so, after our five-mile walk from Bethlehem, Matthias and I arrived and like good Jews, we went first to the Temple. Right away we felt something stirring. The Pharisees were grilling a rabbi, and he fired right back. *It's Jesus of Nazareth*, someone whispered.

"I am the good shepherd," He said. "I know my own and my own know me. In the same way, the Father knows me and I know the Father. And I lay down my life for the sheep."

"Sabba, is he a shepherd like us?" Matthias hung close.

"Apparently so."

More claims and the insulted Pharisees threw up their hands and stormed off.

Then, the oddest thing happened. The rabbi from Nazareth turned His head in our direction and looked right at me. Over the dozens of heads packed between us, His eyes grabbed mine and He smiled like He knew me. He cut through the crowd to get to us.

"How are things in Bethlehem?" He asked.

"How did You know that's our home, rabbi?"

"It's always been your home, hasn't it, David? And before you, it was your father's home, may He rest in peace. Good to meet you, Matthias."

Matthias couldn't say a word and my tongue was no better.

"You heard me say, I am the Good Shepherd, yes? You, too, are a good shepherd, David. From now on, follow My voice. Let me lead you in the straight path and to the pastures. Let Me restore your soul."

He looked at me directly, reading my thoughts. And perhaps because He saw my small faith, He smiled again and nodded as if to say, "Yes, you were with me the night of my birth; you heard the angel's announcement. You are right to believe I am your Messiah."

In that moment, years of cynicism melted away. Yes, it was Him. Somehow I knew His voice. The Psalter swelled in my soul, *"ADONAI is my shepherd; I have everything I need."*

He talked with us a little longer then turned to go. A shadow fell over His smile as He said shalom.

"You of all people know, David, that a good shepherd lays down his life for his sheep. We stand here in the temple—a place where a sheep has no value to God other than its life. Remember that."

(For more in this imaginative story, see part 1 on page XX and part 3 on page XX.)

Tomorrow: *One on one with Jesus and His disciples on retreat*

 Let's talk about it:

1. Did you look for Jesus or did He find you first? Share how you first knew He was a Savior.
2. Do you know the Psalm 23, quoted here? It's a great one to memorize and have ready when you need to be reminded of what Jesus, the Shepherd does for us.

DAY 30

Rock

The One who storms hell

And Jesus went on with his disciples to the villages of Caesarea Philippi. And on the way he asked his disciples, "Who do people say that I am?" And they told him, "John the Baptist; and others say, Elijah; and others, one of the prophets." And he asked them, "But who do you say that I am?" Peter answered him, "You are the Christ." Mark 8:27-29

Everyone needs a place to go to sort things out.

For Jesus, that place was Caesarea Philippi—which would be a shock to everyone back home. This town, forty miles north of Galilee at the base of Mount Hermon, was Gentile country. Beautiful, yes, but Caesarea Philippi was also called "the Gates of Hell," as the grotto from which a stream flowed was considered the entrance to the underworld. Pagan worshippers did despicable things as worship of demons in the shrines carved in the rock cliff walls.

What a curious place for Jesus to take His disciples on a retreat.

These were confusing times for the disciples. Three years now following their rabbi, they witnessed miracle after miracle—Jesus proving His power over demons, over nature, over death and disease. They sat at His feet re-learning what it means to please God. The crowds swelled in number and fervor around Jesus. Even on this retreat, the disciples half-expected Him to announce a plan to overthrow Rome. *That's what everyone expects the Messiah to do. And He is the Messiah, right?*

It was finally time for Jesus to help them get that right, so He took them from the crowds and into the quiet. He first asked, "Who do the crowds think I am?" *John the Baptist or Elijah come back to life. Maybe Jeremiah or another prophet.*

"Who do *you* think I am?" And the beautiful, bold Peter confessed for them all, "You are the Christ, the Son of the living God."

Jesus blessed him and said, "You've been listening to my Father! He told you this secret of who I really am. And now I will tell you who you *really* are. You are Peter, a rock." (Can you picture Him gesturing around Him to the rock wall behind them?) Even in an evil world, Jesus then promised to build His church. And "not even the gates of hell will keep it out." And it made sense to the disciples why they were in Caesarea Philippi.

But what Jesus said next made no sense at all.

"Now I must go to Jerusalem, be rejected, suffer and be killed, and then rise again." *What?*

"Never, Jesus! That's crazy talk!" Peter, still processing Jesus' full identity, stepped over the line. For three years, Jesus was human to them. Now they realized He is also God. It made no sense why He would die.

But Jesus said that's what a real Messiah does. He saves. His death for us will be the only way we can be saved.

Jesus told them He planned it this way before the world was even created. That's how long He has waited to buy back His own. If He is your Savior, then You've been on His mind since then.

His focus now was to put that plan in play. He's ready to pay the price. His choice to die made perfect sense.

Tomorrow: *One on one with Jesus and Moses and Elijah*

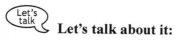 **Let's talk about it:**

1. Who do you think Jesus is?
2. Why was it important that Jesus told them who He was and what He was going to do there in Caesarea Phillipi? How is that place like our culture today?

DAY 31

Glory

The One who was and will be

Jesus took with him Peter and James and John, and led them up a high mountain by themselves. And he was transfigured before them, and his clothes became radiant, intensely white, as no one on earth could bleach them. And there appeared to them Elijah with Moses, and they were talking with Jesus. Mark 9:2-4

Jesus' time on earth was at its peak. Starting now, all roads cascade in a fast, downhill spiral to Jerusalem and the Cross. In three months, Jesus will lay down His life.

Perhaps saying it out loud to the disciples made it all the more real to Him. Today, Jesus needed His Father—He needed confirmation and clarity. He needed strength to continue with the plan. Perhaps most of all, He needed comfort. Perspective. Yes, He knew the reason He left heaven for earth was to die for the sins of the world, but now it's here and in His humanity, the prospect overwhelmed Him. So with His three closest men, Jesus climbed a mountain to pray.

After the hike up the mountain, Peter, James, and John took a nap, and Jesus took to His knees. Suddenly, a light burst from His face and His clothes flashed with electricity. For a few, brief, shining moments, time and space shifted. This Jesus, bursting with light, became the Jesus He was before He came to earth. The burden of His humanity momentarily lifted and Jesus stood there as He always has existed in His glory.

But He wasn't alone. His Father sent two servants to help Him, just like He had three years ago when angels cared for Jesus after forty days of wilderness testing. This time, the Father sent Moses and Elijah.

Yes, the same Moses who 1300 years before led God's people out of Egypt and who carried the ten commandments down another mountain—*that* Moses. Moses had asked God if he could glimpse His glory and now here he is, standing with Jesus in His glory (and finally *in* the Promised Land.)

And Elijah, the courageous prophet, who 850 years before stood for God in a wicked generation and on a mountain just south of here called down fire on evil, and stopped the rain on command, and for whom God sent a chariot of fire to uber him directly to heaven.

They were the rock stars of Jewish history. But for Jesus, they were messengers from home. They knew who He was, where He'd come from, and where He was going. And for a few short moments, they stood with Him and strengthened Him.

Perhaps they reminded this weary Warrior of the joy ahead. On the cross a few weeks from now, He will defeat death. He will stomp evil and sin under His feet—a plan revealed in the Garden of Eden. Someday He will present His blood-bought believing ones to His Father and bring them home with Him. Just the reminder of it all renewed Jesus' courage.

By now, the disciples were awake and witnessing the dazzling scene. They're amazed to see their heroes from history. But a glimpse of Jesus' glory sent them to their faces. The awe could have killed them.

Then a cloud shrouded the mountaintop and a voice thundered, *"This is my Son, whom I love; with Him I am well pleased. Listen to Him!"* The same voice, the same approval Jesus heard from His

Father at the beginning of His ministry now strengthened Him for the final run. Recharged, Jesus was ready for what waited for Him in Jerusalem.

And just like that, the mountaintop was dark and quiet again. Jesus reached down and helped His stunned friends to their feet. Wide-eyed and quiet, they looked at Him like for the first time.

Once you see Jesus for who He really is, can you ever see life or yourself the same way again?

Tomorrow: *One on one with Jesus and a grateful sinner*

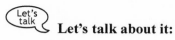 **Let's talk about it:**

1. What Old Testament person would you like to meet?
2. How is your understanding of who Jesus really is growing?

DAY 32

Forgiven
The One who sees our soul

A woman of the city, who was a sinner, when she learned that he was reclining at table in the Pharisee's house, brought an alabaster flask of ointment, and standing behind him at his feet, weeping, she began to wet his feet with her tears and wiped them with the hair of her head and kissed his feet and anointed them with the ointment. Now when the Pharisee who had invited him saw this, he said to himself, "If this man were a prophet, he would have known who and what sort of woman this is who is touching him, for she is a sinner."
Luke 7:36-39

"Party-crasher" was hardly the worst name she had been called. Other names—like whore, slut, prostitute—hurt way worse. No one grows up aspiring to such a vocation. And no one outlives it.

It's better than starving, some would justify. She wasn't so sure. When circumstances turned on her, selling what should have been treasured was the only way she knew to survive.

The day she crashed the party, she knew something the men in the room missed. She knew better than them, apparently, how much she needed to be forgiven. Off-screen somewhere recently, she had found that mercy in Jesus.

So never mind the rude chatter that swept the room, Jesus saw her. Jesus saved her.

Thank You for rescuing me, Jesus. For bending down when no one else cared. You took this beat up life and made me new. Forgiveness: received. The beauty of it made her weep.

And Jesus didn't stop her. He knew everything about her, what "kind of woman she was" and it moved Him even more. *"Her sins, which are many, are forgiven,"* He said to the room. She used to be bought cheap, then He bought her back. And the only appropriate place for her to be right now was at His feet.

But if that wasn't shocking enough to the room, she unfurled her long hair (the cultural equivalent of undressing), and covered Jesus' feet with her kisses and tears and dried them with her hair.

Normally, a host would see to the common courtesy of washing his guests' tired and dusty feet. Jesus was quick to meet His host's indignant, accusing stare with, *"No one else washed My feet . . ."*

Everything about her humble act told Jesus she understood the depth of her sin and knew His mercy went deeper still. She was the only person in the room who understood who she was without His forgiveness and who she is now because of it.

We learn quite a lesson in her beautiful act: the intensity of our love for Jesus is in direct proportion to our realization of how much we've been forgiven.

Tomorrow: *One on one with Jesus in the dark*

182

Let's talk about it:

1. It's a private thing—how much we need to be forgiven. When the truth of your sin humbles you, what do you want to do?

2. What do you love about Jesus in this encounter?

DAY 33

In the Dark
The One who is your life

When Mary came to where Jesus was and saw him, she fell at his feet, saying to him, "Lord, if you had been here, my brother would not have died." When Jesus saw her weeping, and the Jews who had come with her also weeping, he was deeply moved in his spirit and greatly troubled. And he said, "Where have you laid him?" They said to him, "Lord, come and see." Jesus wept. John 11:32-35

God said *no*. Or worse, He said nothing. You're praying for something important, urgent. Specific. Even a matter of life and death. You pound on heaven's front door, but the silence crushes you as what concerns you slips away.

Jesus had best friends in Bethany, all in one family. He stayed with them whenever He was in town. The long evenings over Martha's good cooking and Mary's gentle ways brought Him relief from the stresses of ministry. He and Lazarus shared the same humor and could laugh hard, till the sisters rolled their eyes and laughed just at them.

Jesus was on the east side of the Jordan, 20 miles away, when Lazarus suddenly got sick. Martha, being Martha, sent word to Jesus by the fastest messenger—they needed His help, *now*. He healed plenty others, *come heal your friend*. She and Mary watched the road, expecting Him to show up any minute.

Just like us. "Pray about it," people say and so we do. "Trust Him," and we try. Then nothing happens—and sometimes people die.

Just like Lazarus did. When Jesus shows up four days later, He doesn't even explain Himself. Neither does God when He doesn't seem to be there when you need Him. You're left in the dark.

"Lord, if you had been here, my brother would not have died." Martha first, then Mary said it to Jesus, maybe the same way they had reassured each other while they waited. *Jesus will come and Lazarus won't die.* (But then he did.)

Their grief touched Jesus even though all along His plan was to surprise them (especially Lazarus). A quiet tear rolled down His face as He stood in front of his friend's tomb.

Look at how Jesus loved him, some remarked. *Yeah? So why didn't He come?*

Better question: Why did Jesus cry when He knew Lazarus would be back at the dinner table that night? Was He sorry for what His delay put them through? Maybe on a deeper level He grieved the personal cost of sin. Or was He thinking of His own death just a couple weeks away?

His face still wet with tears, Jesus did the unimaginable. He called Lazarus back to life. In one moment. Everyone's grief turned to shock, turned to joy. *What?!* With His two words, *'Come out!,'* wide-eyed, Lazarus shuffles out of the tomb, wrapped like a mummy in grave clothes. His story wasn't over after all.

Jesus told us to walk with Him by faith. Usually the way He trains us to do that is to put us in the dark. Only then will we reach out our hand and take His.

He told Martha in her grief, *"I am the resurrection and the life. The one who believes in me will live, even though they die."*

The wait forces us to trust Him. Someday He will explain why.

Tomorrow: *One on one with Jesus catching people being faithful*

 Let's talk about it:

1. Have you ever thought a story was over, then God did something remarkable?
2. If you're waiting on God for something today, how do you relate to this story?

══ DAY 34 ══

Snapshots
The One who notices you

Which of these three, do you think, proved to be a neighbor to the man who fell among the robbers?" He said, "The one who showed him mercy." And Jesus said to him, "You go, and do likewise." Luke 10:36-37

Jesus had as much time as everyone else, yet He was never in a hurry. He took the time to notice people, even the ones others overlooked. His favorite moments were when He caught His own being faithful. And when He did . . .

. . . JESUS REWARDED THE CREATIVE ONES. MARK 2:1-12

After Jesus brushed off the dirt and straw from His hair and shoulders, He likely looked up and laughed. Four young men peeked through the hole in the roof. Their bold belief in Jesus gave them the idea to lower their paralyzed friend down on a blanket in front of Him. "We couldn't get in the door," they said half-apologetically. Crowds packed the place. "And our friend needs You."
To what lengths will you go to introduce your friends to Jesus?

Madman. Demoniac. On the other side of the Sea of Galilee, a 'kid next door' had morphed into a foaming-at-the-mouth monster. But even with the legion of demons controlling his mind and body, the kid ran to Jesus the second He stepped on shore. Jesus knew his whole story and how the demons raged inside him. He couldn't be happier to command the whole filthy legion out of the young man (and into a herd of pigs nearby—who then ran off a cliff). Restored, the young man wanted to join Jesus' group, but Jesus told him instead, *go tell your neighbors what I've done for you.* When the young man did, it brought the town such excitement to hear about Jesus that they completely changed the story they told about him.
Instead of "victim," what do people say about you since Jesus changed your identity?

. . . JESUS HONORED THE ONE HATED FOR HIS RACE. LUKE 10:25-37

In Jesus' day, you'd never call a Samaritan "good." Jews called them *half-breed, heathen, unclean.* Yet that didn't matter to the Samaritan who inspired Jesus' parable. On the treacherous road out of Jericho when the Samaritan came upon a beaten and robbed Jewish man left for dead, he stopped and cared for him like he would a neighbor, even at his own expense—unlike the racist, religious men who stepped over the suffering man on their way to worship in Jerusalem. Perhaps because the Samaritan had tasted man's hatred could he instead serve up kindness to the broken one God loves. Suffering levels us all to the place of mercy.
Who in your world needs you to show them God's mercy?

. . . JESUS MULTIPLIED THE SMALL GIFT OF A SMALL BOY. MARK 6:30-44

No one in the crowd knew it was *his* lunch that fed them that day. No one else's mother sent their boy out with a snack of sardines and barley crackers—or at least no one else was willing to share theirs.

But neither did anyone else hear the Teacher say, *"thanks, lad"* as He tussled his hair. With a mischievous grin, perhaps the Lord even leaned down and whispered—*just watch what I'll do with your gift.* C.S. Lewis once said, "He who has God and everything else has no more than he who has God only." The generous boy who had only one gift to offer God got to be used by God to treat 15,000 people to lunch.

* *If you're willing for God to use you, what could He do with your one small gift?*

Think about this: at the same time Jesus took these quiet snapshots of faith, He kept atoms spinning. Tides turning. Axis tilting. Gravity pulling. While the Creator and Sustainer of the universe keeps everything in its place, He notices every act of faith you do today. When you walk with Him, it makes Him so glad.

Tomorrow: *One on one with Jesus and His days to come*

 Let's talk about it:

1. To what lengths will you go to introduce your friends to Jesus?
2. Who in your world needs you to show them God's mercy?
3. What could God do with your one small gift, if you're willing for Him to do anything?

DAY 35

I Am

The One who will die for you

Not that I have already obtained this or am already perfect, but I press on to make it my own, because Christ Jesus has made me his own. Brothers, I do not consider that I have made it my own. But one thing I do: forgetting what lies behind and straining forward to what lies ahead, I press on toward the goal for the prize of the upward call of God in Christ Jesus. Philippians 3:12-14

You awake? Me, too. It's the last night on the road for our team, way past midnight. We're in Jericho, camping in a friends' stable before tomorrow's final 20-mile hike up to Jerusalem. From what Rabbi says, we're heading straight into a storm and we're not going to make it out alive—at least not all of us.

Imagine talking with John, the disciple who lived another 60 years after that night. Listen to how John might have reflected on the events near the end of Jesus' ministry years.

Back when I was a young man, people called my brother James and me, "sons of thunder." Back in that day, I walked with God. For most of those days, we wouldn't have guessed Jesus was really God. He was our rabbi; He was my mentor and friend.

That night before we went up to Jerusalem the last time together, I woke in the third watch and noticed Jesus' empty bedroll. Everyone was asleep, but I found Him up and not far away, kneeling against a boulder. Praying.

When I close my eyes, I'm there again, under the stars. Or on the lake shore with James and dad. Or on the trail with the other disciples—all of them gone now. I can still taste the wine that moments before had been water. And smell Mary's oil—the fragrance carried through the room.

Sometimes I still hear Jesus' voice.

I am the light of the world, He said . . . A light—to rescue those whose sin keeps them in a dark place. Like the man Jesus rescued from demons, and the woman at the well.

I am the door . . . The only way in—for those looking for God's greater plan. Like Nicodemus and Nathaniel—sincere yet searching in the wrong place.

I am the bread of life . . . Satisfaction—for those who hunger for God's kind of life. Like those in the crowds who experienced a miracle but embraced a Savior.

I am the way. . . Truth. Life.—for every follower like us who believe Jesus is the road... the only way to heaven.

I am the resurrection . . . Eternal life—for everyone who turns to Him when life fails and hope dies.

Everything Jesus said about Himself came back to us later.

The last memory I have of Jesus from that night was Him sitting in the moonlight, His soul at rest, and His hand comforting a lamb curled beside Him. The lamb, loved by the family and kept as a pet, would the next week be taken to temple for Passover. An acceptable sacrifice.

And so would Jesus.

Next, walk with Jesus on His way to the Cross—the Lamb of God who takes away the sin of the world. Witness the greatest gift you've ever been given as it happened in that final week.

 Let's talk about it:

1. Which of the five "I am..." statements do you feel drawn to? Why?
2. Of all the people you met one on one here, who do you remember best? Better yet, what do you remember about Jesus?

PART 3
ONE ON ONE WITH JESUS – IN HIS PASSION

Everything beautiful, precious and epic about your relationship with God hangs on what Jesus did in the days surrounding His death and resurrection. These steps leading to the Cross are hard to watch—by design. Yet Jesus wants you to know nobody took His life; He laid it down willingly. For us. Get the complete story here—and a glimpse at what's ahead for everyone who follows Jesus.

PART 3

One on One with Jesus – in His Passion

DAY 1

For the Joy

The One who finishes what He starts

Therefore, since we are surrounded by so great a cloud of witnesses, let us also lay aside every weight, and sin which clings so closely, and let us run with endurance the race that is set before us, [2] looking to Jesus, the founder and perfecter of our faith, who for the joy that was set before him endured the cross, despising the shame, and is seated at the right hand of the throne of God. Hebrews 12:1-2

Jesus finishes what He starts.

When we witnessed Jesus' birth, we met people in Jesus' backstory. He stepped into time, put on skin, and showed us God's love, the ultimate Christmas gift.

Through His ministry years, we watched Jesus heal and teach and connect with people. We learned how to *"love each other the way I have loved you."*

But never before or since can we see love better personified than in Jesus' walk to the cross. Those are hard days to watch. We want to look away. We cringe at the injustice and agony.

But Jesus wants us to see something different. He wants us to know . . .

- That every second of His suffering was by design.
- That nobody took His life, but He laid it down willingly.
- That the Cross was the plan all along.

Actually, you were on His mind in these days. Hebrews 12:1 says Jesus endured the cross because it gave Him joy to pay off your debt, allowing you to live with Him forever. If we stand alone before God, our sin condemns us to hell. But Jesus' body broken and innocent blood shed paid what God's holiness requires. Jesus' sacrifice covers our sin, every single one.

In the coming days you will witness Jesus:

Misunderstood	Betrayed	Deserted
Arrested	Denied	Beaten
Tried	Mocked	Crucified

It will feel like a train off its track. But don't believe it; Jesus was right on mission. In any moment, God the Father could have rescued Him. But something bigger was going on.

As we go *One on One with Jesus in His Passion*, don't get caught up in the horror of Jesus' murder, instead, embrace the extravagance of His gift.

"Grasp how wide and long and high and deep is Jesus' love, and to know this love that surpasses knowledge—that you may live full lives, full in the fullness of God."

This is Jesus finishing what He started. Celebrate the end goal: us with Him forever.

But stick around. Until that final day, He's still working on us, and in us. *Until then, be confident of this: that He who began a good work in you will carry it on to completion until the day of Christ Jesus.*

Let's see how in the days ahead.

Tomorrow: *One on one with Jesus as it begins*

 Let's talk about it:

1. What do you hope to experience in a new way this Passion season?

2. Does it change anything about the Easter story for you to think about the long story that God had in mind.

DAY 2

Jericho Road

The One who worshipped

When the days drew near for him to be taken up, he set his face to go to Jerusalem. Luke 9:51

It was the first of many lasts for Jesus. Today He walks the road from Jericho to Jerusalem for the last time. The switchback canyon path rises 3,300 feet out of an oasis through treacherous terrain, from Jericho (820 ft. *below* sea level) to Jerusalem (2,500 ft. *above* sea level).

As a good Jew, Jesus walked this road at least six times every year going to and from Galilee to celebrate the feasts of Passover, Pentecost, and Tabernacles. More than 100 times in His lifetime. He knew every turn, every ravine, precipice, and gorge.

Satan once tempted Jesus near here in a wilderness and no doubt tempted Him again on this last climb. If Jesus wanted a way to escape what waited Him, He would have found one. But this road went in one direction—to Jerusalem and to His death. Luke said He "set his face like a flint for Jerusalem."

Ahead of Him waited unimaginable suffering and behind Jesus walked His disciples, arguing over who would be first in the new kingdom.

For 3,000 years, Jewish pilgrims climbed this path. And you know what they did to get their hearts ready to worship in Jerusalem (and maybe to get their minds off the steep climb)? They sang. The Songs of Ascent, Psalms 120—134, were written specifically to be sung as you walk up this road.

Picture Jesus and His disciples walking side by side, or sometimes single-file, singing about God. Someone would start a familiar tune and others would join in. Their deep voices harmonized and filled the canyon and cliffs stretching above and below them. They sang:

I lift up my eyes to the hills. From where does my help come?

My help comes from the LORD, who made heaven and earth.

He will not let your foot be moved; he who keeps you will not slumber.

Behold, he who keeps Israel will neither slumber nor sleep. Psalm 121:1-4

Jesus could have avoided Jerusalem and everyone who wanted to kill Him there. He could have turned back anywhere on this road. But instead, He sang about His Father . . . He worshipped.

The reality of what waited ahead was never far from His thoughts—but neither were you. And what He was determined to accomplish in the next few days would change your destiny, even the future of the world.

Today, over the last rise in this road from Jericho, you catch a glimpse of the Old City spread out like a rug. For everyone who loves the Lord, the sight of it brings tears. It's meant to be this way.

Tomorrow: *One on one with Jesus on Palm Sunday*

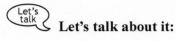 **Let's talk about it:**

1. Do you like to sing songs about God? When/Where is your favorite time and place? What are a few of your go-to songs?
2. What about Jesus' determination changes this "tragic" story?

DAY 3

Hosanna

The One who cried

And when he drew near and saw the city, he wept over it, saying, "Would that you, even you, had known on this day the things that make for peace! But now they are hidden from your eyes. For the days will come upon you, when your enemies will set up a barricade around you and surround you and hem you in on every side and tear you down to the ground, you and your children within you. And they will not leave one stone upon another in you, because you did not know the time of your visitation."
Luke 19:41-44

Jesus cried twice in the weeks leading to the cross. The first was when He stood with Martha and Mary at their brother Lazarus' new grave.

We're just told, "Jesus wept." We get to witness a very private moment for Jesus. This word "wept," *dakruo*, describes the quiet grief that streams down your face. The more common word for weeping is *klaio*, "a loud wail." John 11:33 says Mary *klaio*, "wailed," as she stood there beside Jesus.

Jesus also cried Palm Sunday, the first day of Passover week. This is the day when people chose their sacrificial lambs. Fittingly, Jesus made a very grand entrance into Jerusalem that day in a way that fulfilled Old Testament prophecies. But this time His tears weren't quiet at all. He *klaio*.

He wailed the full ride down the Mount of Olives, across the Kidron Valley, and into the city through the Sheep Gate. The tassels on His prayer shawl drug the ground and got stained with the blood that drained from the countless lamb sacrifices offered high above on the Temple altar. The wind carried the scent of burning flesh mingled with the people's cries for a political Messiah—but not a personal Savior.

People searched for salvation everywhere except where they could find it. That's why Jesus cried. He wept at their loud "Hosannas" because they missed the point. They shouted, "Save us, O LORD! Blessed is he who comes in the name of the LORD!," echoing Psalm 118, promising political freedom from the Messiah.

Ironically, the Pharisees got it. They demanded Jesus stop the people from blessing Him as a king. He answered, "If they were silent, the stones would shout." Jesus *will* be praised.

But the people cried for a king, not a personal Savior. The next few days would settle it. On Friday the city would slam the door on Jesus's offer of salvation.

If only you believed what I say, Jesus wept. Perhaps the reality of their rejection and all it will mean to Israel's future sunk in. Within one generation, Jerusalem will lay in rubble, demolished. Today, Jesus set the plan in motion as He gave His enemies the upper hand.

In the moment you'd think He would cry for Himself, Jesus weeps for all the sheep He wants to save—yet who run from His rescue. He is the way home they will not take. The truth they will not believe. The life they will not accept.

The thought of it made Him openly sob.

Tomorrow: *One on one with Jesus at a party*

Let's talk about it:

1. When was the last time you cried? What prompted your tears?

2. Misunderstanding causes a lot of frustration, tears. How do people misunderstand Jesus' offer today?

DAY 4

Beautiful

The One who will die

But Jesus, aware of this, said to them, "Why do you trouble the woman? For she has done a beautiful thing to me. For you always have the poor with you, but you will not always have me. In pouring this ointment on my body, she has done it to prepare me for burial. Truly, I say to you, wherever this gospel is proclaimed in the whole world, what she has done will also be told in memory of her."
Matthew 26:10-13

Jesus said He would die in Jerusalem, but every one of His friends assured Him He wouldn't. All except one.

Only Mary of Bethany accepted the news. Only she believed and grieved what He said would happen. Only she valued their last, precious days together. All the special evenings Jesus spent in their home, their conversations, her flashes of faith—all these moments were ending. In the greater grief, this was her private sorrow.

Time raced down a runaway track towards this weekend. Jesus must have also felt the urgency. This was His week to stand face-to-face with evil personified. The weight of approaching grief hung over Him. He would be dead by Friday.

Yet on this Saturday night He gathered with His favorite people. Simon (formerly known as the leper) threw Him a dinner party and invited His disciples and friends. Into this gathering walked Mary.

She came with a mission. With a year's salary, Mary had bought an alabaster jar of spikenard perfume. With this outrageously expensive offering in hand, she stood above her friend who sat low at a table, and broke the bottle's narrow neck. Usually sprinkled a drop at a time, she poured the oil over Jesus' head. The undiluted nard streamed down His hair, then shoulders, down His chest. It's what a loved one does to prepare a body for burial.

The symbolism was not lost on Jesus.

Mary had developed the habit of breaking cultural rules. First, she sat at Jesus' feet while He taught, something no respectable woman would dare do. It angered her sister; but it pleased the Lord. Now, she poured out this exquisite oil; it incensed the greedy disciple, and confused the others. But again, it pleased the Lord.

"Let her alone," Jesus defended her. "She's doing something significant and wonderful for Me."

Mission accomplished. She could not stop the evil ready to swallow Him. Instead she expressed this tenderness while He was still with them. Her tears told her sorrow. Her sacrifice spoke of His impending death. She didn't try to stop Him, even if she could. She just let Him be her Savior.

So strong was this oil Mary emptied out that it would cling to Jesus' hair and skin for days. Perhaps smelling its lingering aroma as He sweat and bled on Friday through the hours of torture and dying was His one trace of comfort. The sweet fragrance of love poured out—as He did the same.

Tomorrow: *One on one with Jesus on Thursday night.*

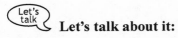

Let's talk about it:

1. How do you think you would have reacted to Jesus' news that He was going to die?
2. Was Mary's offering worth it? How about the sacrifice you're making today for Jesus?—worth it?

DAY 5

Passover Lamb

The One who was provided for you

Isaac said to his father Abraham, "My father!" And he said, "Here I am, my son." He said, "Behold, the fire and the wood, but where is the lamb for a burnt offering?" Abraham said, "God will provide for himself the lamb for a burnt offering, my son." So they went both of them together. Genesis 22:7-8

Thursday evening, late.

Wine filled their cups as the disciples ate the special Passover meal. Their last dinner together. He was so glad to share it with them, Jesus said. Arms outstretched, He lifted the cup.

"I make a new covenant with you in my blood poured out for you."

*Blood poured out to get to God. . . .*They've heard of this sacrifice before.

1800 B.C. *"Here's the wood, but <u>where's the sacrifice?</u>"*

211

The boy Isaacs's question on Mount Moriah had haunted their stories for generations.

"God Himself will provide a lamb," Father Abraham answered, out of faith and nothing more.

Friday morning, early. Here's the wood.

From a safe distance, the disciples watch the Passover Lamb stretched out on Mount Moriah, now Jerusalem. Same place, centuries apart. *Here's the sacrifice.*

It finally hit them, the Lamb *had been with them* all along.

Forgiveness and mercy pour out, pooled from the One they love . . . who love *them* even more. To pay a price *this* scandalous makes no sense, except for love.

Here, too, is the wood. The bridge—so we can get to God.

Such is the price paid for an eternity with Him.

All on a good Friday morning.

Tomorrow: *One on one with Jesus at dinnertime*

 Let's talk about it:

1. Have you ever connected the stories of Abraham offering Isaac on Mount Moriah with Jesus offering Himself on Calvary? Same place—centuries apart. One a picture. The other a promise kept.
2. "To pay a price this scandalous makes no sense except for love." Agree or disagree?

DAY 6

Proposal

The One who will come for His bride

And he took bread, and when he had given thanks, he broke it and gave it to them, saying, "This is my body, which is given for you. Do this in remembrance of me." And likewise the cup after they had eaten, saying, "This cup that is poured out for you is the new covenant in my blood. Luke 22:19-20

How would you answer this?

For my last meal, I would eat _____(what) with _____ (who).

Jesus would have answered like this:

I want my last meal to be the Passover Seder and I want to eat it with My disciples.

The Seder is the best special occasion of the year for Jewish families. Everything about it reminds them of their heritage. The food, the symbolism, the candles, the wine, the rhetoric, the sequence, the questions—all point to the time God rescued them from slavery in Egypt and set them apart as belonging to Him alone.

This year, no one in that upstairs room realized just how significant this Seder was, except of course, Jesus. He lived under the shadow of the cross, now about 15 hours away. The countdown had begun. Judas had left to alert the Pharisees where Jesus could be found. Jesus likely sensed Satan's presence in the room.

So Jesus stands and raises a cup of wine like a toast. *"This cup is the new covenant in my blood, which is poured out for you." Wait*, the disciples thought, *this doesn't sound like a Seder. This is a marriage proposal!*

When a Jewish man proposed to a woman, he passed her a cup of wine. If she drank from it, she accepted his proposal and they were engaged. With the wine comes a promise—a new covenant. He promises to pay her father the price to take her as his bride. He would then go to his father's house and begin building a suite of rooms for them to make into their home. When the place he prepared for her was ready, he promised to come get her and they would be married that night. She wouldn't know when he would come, so she had to stay ready.

On their last night together before the cross, Jesus proposes to the ones He loves. "This cup is the new covenant in my blood, which is poured out for you." He promises them and every follower after: *I'll pay the price to redeem you. I'll give up my life for you and go my Father's house to prepare a place for you. And one day I will return and bring you to be with me forever.*

On a night reserved for a long, grateful look at the past, Jesus redirected their attention to the future. He completed the picture of the old Passover tradition by pointing to the rescue His own sacrifice would provide the next day.

We do the same every time we observe communion, or the Lord's Supper. When you eat the bread and drink the cup, remember the price Jesus paid and the promise He made to come and take you as His bride.

Though the years may feel long, the days are short till He comes to take us home to be forever with Him. The house is almost ready, and the bridegroom will be coming back any day to get us.

Tomorrow: *One on one with Jesus as He washes feet*

 Let's talk about it:

1. If you could plan it, what would your last meal look like?
2. Next time you eat/drink communion/ the Lord's Supper, remember this marriage proposal Jesus offers you—and the promise still to come.

═══ DAY 7 ═══

Last Supper

The One who washes feet

Jesus, knowing that the Father had given all things into his hands, and that he had come from God and was going back to God, ⁴ rose from supper. He laid aside his outer garments, and taking a towel, tied it around his waist. ⁵ Then he poured water into a basin and began to wash the disciples' feet and to wipe them with the towel that was wrapped around him. John 13:3-6

Everything good in your life with God comes out of humility. Every step backwards is because of pride.

Jesus noticed the disciples' tendency towards self-promotion. *Who was better. Whose throne was closest to Jesus'.* More than locker-room brag, this was ugly pride. Dangerous, even.

Jesus addressed it with them a couple times, but in the urgency of this last day decided to show them, rather than speak to them again about it.

Listen—what's that? Under the loud arguments at the table, the disciples heard water splashing. There was Jesus, His robe off, tying a towel around His waist. With a bowl of water, He knelt beside Matthew and sponged cool water over his ankles. He wiped his foot clean with the towel, and moved on to the next man, perhaps Phillip, maybe Judas. Then John.

Except for the water, the room was silent. They challenged each other for the throne, but nobody fought over the towel. Far from just a profound gesture, this was demeaning work, beneath them all.

But look at Him there. If anyone had a right to be proud, Jesus did. He could dispatch angels to sing about His glory, but instead, here He is, bent over, washing dirty, proud feet.

Hear that water? Let it remind you that the root of every sin you struggle with is pride. You want to be first. It's true for us all.

If you want to be done with that pride and take a step forward in your life in God, do this: get your hands together and cup them like you're holding water. Envision holding your motives, your dreams, everything that drives you forward. Offer them up to the Lord with a prayer something like:

Lord, Your Word says You oppose the proud but give grace to the humble. I know my own pride. I know I naturally choose it every time. But if You tell me to do something, You give me the ability to do it in Your strength. So, help me as I choose by faith to stand before You today. Use the challenges and pain of life to soften my hard heart. Teach me how to walk out Your Word, faithfully, quietly, to please You alone. Help me humble myself. I stand accountable to You for every loose thought, every word spoken, every emotion and impulse nurtured.

Fill me with Your Spirit as I go forward with You. In Jesus' name and because of His example, amen.

Tomorrow: *One on one with Jesus as He says goodbye to His disciples*

Let's talk about it:

1. Go ahead—get your hands together and cup them like you're holding water. Envision holding your motives, your dreams, everything that drives you forward. Offer them up to the Lord.

2. Write out your own prayer of surrender that you can return to the next time you struggle with pride.

DAY 8

The Promise

The One who is preparing us for a place

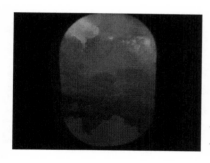

"Let not your hearts be troubled. Believe in God; believe also in me. In my Father's house are many rooms. If it were not so, would I have told you that I go to prepare a place for you? And if I go and prepare a place for you, I will come again and will take you to myself, that where I am you may be also." John 14:1-3

What are we going to do now?—We think that when we're grieving.

Maybe that's what the disciples thought when Jesus told them He was going away. They felt like He was deserting them. He's going, but they're staying. *What are we going to do now?*

What's worse, Jesus wasn't just going away—He said He was going to die. The one they sat with now at the table would be gone tomorrow. Dead. It was too much for them to process.

Behind our masks, most of us nurse a troubled heart. Most likely, the thing you're worrying about right now is wrapped in fear or anxiety or guilt or frustration.

Jesus knows all about our problems. He knew the disciples were turning into rough waters. Let's sit with Him at the table as they finish up their last meal together. Let Him speak to your heart today, too.

"Don't let your heart be troubled; You trust God—now trust Me." Jesus doesn't skirt the issue. Hard times are coming, *but I will help you through them. Trust me.*

Let me tell you what's ahead, He said. *I'm going home and getting the house ready. At the right time, I'll come back to get you and we'll be together again, all in my Father's house.*

Hope. There it is right in the middle of the heartache. He's saying, *It's not always going to be this hard. You won't always feel alone. Your heart won't always break. Sin won't always be a struggle. A day is coming when we'll be together again in My Father's house.*

The invitation is ours, too. While Jesus prepares that place for us, He's also preparing us for that place. Two construction projects are happening right now.

Death and pain, even failure and crushing—somehow, they're all part of that construction process. They're getting us ready for life beyond this atmosphere, weaning us a bit at a time from earth, preparing our lungs to breathe heavenly air. Perhaps you've seen that readiness in a saint sitting on heaven's doorstep.

You can sure see it in Jesus that night around the table.

He wasn't thinking about the pain He'd face in the morning. He was thinking about another morning, around a larger table, when He'll sit with His disciples again. And we will be there, too. And His eyes will dance when He greets us, one by one. *Welcome home. Your room is ready. I can't wait to show you around.*

That day is coming, just wait and see. It was part of the joy set before Him that helped Jesus endure the cross the next day.

It can be part of the joy set before us here and now, to help us on our way home.

Tomorrow: *One on one with Jesus, the way*

Let's talk about it:

1. How does it make you feel to know Jesus understands your grief / anxiety / frustrations, etc?

2. "While Jesus prepares that place for us, He's also preparing us for that place." How do you think He's preparing you?

DAY 9

The Road

The One who is the only way

In my Father's house are many rooms. If it were not so, would I have told you that I go to prepare a place for you?[b] And if I go and prepare a place for you, I will come again and will take you to myself, that where I am you may be also. [4] And you know the way to where I am going."[c] Thomas said to him, "Lord, we do not know where you are going. How can we know the way?" Jesus said to him, "I am the way, and the truth, and the life. No one comes to the Father except through me. John 14:2-6

You can tell a lot about a person by the road they choose. Ultimately, that road determines where you end up.

When Jesus said goodbye to His disciples a few hours before He was arrested, He said, "I'm going away, but you know the way to where I'm going." They looked at Him like deer in headlights—*if we don't know where You're going, how can we know the way?*

Like on cue, Jesus answers, *"Follow Me—I am the way."* Then He puts the whole gospel in a nutshell: "I am the way, the truth, and the life. No one comes to the Father except through Me." You want to know how to get to God? *I am the way.* Literally, I am *the road.*

A few short years later, all of Jesus' followers were called, "Followers of *the Way.*" Jesus is the road you choose. He is the way you follow.

"He is the way" is an old metaphor made new. In the Old Testament, when the children of Israel wandered the Negev desert out of Egypt, God used a fire at night and a cloud by day "to show *the way* (or *the road)* they should go."

You probably know the promise in Proverbs 3:6, "In all your *ways,* acknowledge Him and He will make your path/*road* straight."

The prophet Isaiah pleaded with us to walk the "highway of holiness," a road reserved for people following God. All Old Testament "roads" were fulfilled when Jesus declared Himself to be *"The Road. . .* the Truth, and the Life" and asked us to walk with Him.

If you want to follow Jesus, pray like Moses did. He asked God, "let me *walk Your road,* that I may know You . . ." (Exodus 33:13). If you walk God's road, you'll learn God's ways—and over a lifetime, that path takes you home.

Tomorrow: *One on one with the One who prays for you*

Let's talk about it:

1. "The road you walk determines the life you'll live." Agree/ Disagree? Why?
2. If you like to take notes in your Bible, circle the word "way" in these verses and pencil in the word "road." (Exodus 33:13, Proverbs 3:6, Isaiah 35:8, John 14:6)

DAY 10

Intercessor

The One who prays for you

When Jesus had spoken these words, he lifted up his eyes to heaven, and said, "Father, the hour has come; glorify your Son that the Son may glorify you, since you have given him authority over all flesh, to give eternal life to all whom you have given him. And this is eternal life, that they know you, the only true God, and Jesus Christ whom you have sent. John 17:1-3

What if you knew Jesus was on His knees in the next room, praying for you?

On the night before He died, Jesus was exactly where He wanted to be—with His disciples. They sat and talked and ate together till almost midnight. Before some turned in and a few went with Him to Gethsemane, Jesus led them in prayer.

Really, He let them eavesdrop while He talked with His Father. He didn't have to pray out loud, but He did because He wanted them to hear His heart. John 17 captures it—the longest prayer in the Bible yet you can read it in three minutes.

If you really want to know someone, listen to them pray. You find out quickly God cares less about eloquent words or your posture or even perfect doctrine. God listens for your heart.

On that important night before the cross, Jesus first prays for Himself. The hour had come He and His Father set in eternity past for Jesus to pay for our sins. By this time tomorrow, Jesus will be in a grave; His work of salvation complete. Jesus talks about this future as if it has already happened. He knows His mission will be a success. So as He turns in His report, Jesus asks His Father to restore their relationship—back to how it had been before Bethlehem. Jesus wants His glory back.

Next, Jesus prays for the men and women who sat around Him. He intercedes for them as a teacher prays for His students. God gave them to Him, now He asks God to protect them and keep them strong, to keep their hearts focused, and to keep them loving and persevering in Him. *Please, guard their souls.*

Then, Jesus intercedes for us. "I am praying for them *for they are yours.*" (Wow!) He asks God to help us live set apart to Him—to help us put Him first. He asks for God to help us remember every day we belong to Him. He asks God to help us love each other and to show the world what it means to love God together.

Jesus still prays for us. With great joy, "He lives to intercede with God on our behalf," (Hebrews 7:25). Right now He's sitting at God's right hand, asking His Father to meet every one of your needs (Romans 8:34).

So it's true—at this moment, Jesus really is in the next room praying for you. Knowing you better than you know yourself—what you need or want, where you're strong, where you lack—and loving you more than words, Jesus acts as your go-between with God, our Father.

Stop and think about that. Does this feed your confidence and joy today? What step of faith might you be willing to try now that you know Jesus is behind you?

Tomorrow: *One on one with God in the garden*

Let's talk about it:

1. How does it make you feel knowing that Jesus is praying for you this moment? What does it change in your thinking?
2. Rehearse the amazing truths from John 17 by telling someone about them. What does Jesus pray for Himself? What does He ask for us and for His disciples?

DAY 11

Gethsemane

The One who said 'yes' to God

In the days of his flesh, Jesus offered up prayers and supplications, with loud cries and tears, to him who was able to save him from death, and he was heard because of his reverence.
Hebrews 5:7

It feels like it's just too much to ask. We each have a limit, our own limit. What God asks of us feels too hard. Not that He actually asks—because who would ever agree to failure or illness or suffering for a child or faithfulness to an impossible spouse? Who would say "yes" to a hurt that won't go away; a heavy burden to carry the rest of your life? Maybe it's the thought of living life alone that's too much. Or in danger. Or with an empty place at your family's table. He didn't ask you if He could write this into your story but He asks you to trust Him now that it is.

That's Jesus in the Garden. If you wonder if Jesus ever felt His back against a wall, look no further than among the trees of Gethsemane. There He is on the ground, His face in the dirt, His fist full of gravel and grass, His mind breaking at the thought of

227

what's next for Him. Here is Jesus in the most honest moment of His humanity.

"Father, is there another way?" Could the Father's sovereignty give Him another option? He didn't pray 'save Me from this hour.' To escape now would be to run from why He came. But this plan, this way, in that moment, seemed too much.

More than physical agony, Jesus likely feared the spiritual. What if in the next hours He disqualified Himself as Savior and in the end all that happened was His own death? No salvation for us; no resurrection for Him. Just death.

Could there be another way? The answer: "No." It was clear.

"But I will help you." It was compassionate.

Jesus kept praying, but it changed to "I want what You want." His submission became the tipping point.

God then sent an angel to strengthen Jesus for this battle to the death. Like He had done in the wilderness after Satan's testing, the Father did again for Jesus in the garden, perhaps again interrupting Satan's taunting. We'll never know how deep the waters Jesus crossed nor how dark the night He passed through. Or how gruesome the crime He endured in the morning. All we know is God helped Jesus in the hour He needed it.

Don't you know He'll do the same for you? The answer to your cry to get you out of this crucible may be "no." But then He promises, "but I will help you." The condition for His rescue is your willingness to say to God—"I want what You want for me."

In every test, a bigger issue is at stake. Will you roll onto Him what is too heavy for you? For Jesus in Gethsemane, it took humble faith to say "yes" to His Father's choice, even to death on a cross. But because Jesus honored God, God answered Him. And His unwavering obedience kept Jesus from being swallowed by death, explains Hebrews 5:7.

By the time Jesus was done praying, He had confirmation of His mission's success. How do we know? Hebrews 12:2 tells us, "For the joy that was set before Him, He endured the cross."

If you will say "yes" to God in the crucible you face today, He will help you. And somewhere in the process, you'll find Him to be worth it all.

Tomorrow: *One on one with Jesus who washed the traitor's feet*

 Let's talk about it:

Have you ever felt like what God was asking of you was too much? What did you do? How did you pray?

1. How does Jesus' example of humble faith, "to say "yes" to His Father's choice" inspire you to say 'yes' to what God is asking of you?
2. Tell a story about how God helped you through something hard.

═══ DAY 12 ═══

Judas

The One who washed the traitor's feet

The Word became flesh and made his dwelling among us. We have seen his glory, the glory of the one and only Son, who came from the Father, full of grace and truth. John 1:14

He's the most notorious villain in the story. The one who pretended to believe, pretended to follow, pretended to be Jesus' *talmadim*, but in the end, he was just a fake. He was one of the twelve chosen disciples, yet today, people don't even name their dogs Judas.

Who knows why Judas joined Jesus' group. Was it for the glory? Did he think Jesus was the political Messiah who would break Rome's stranglehold on Israel? Was it for the money? *Money is always a good idea*, he thought.

Think of your favorite stories from the Gospels and look for Judas' face in the background. When Jesus raised the dead, Judas watched. When Jesus walked on water, Judas sat in the boat. When Jesus called out demons, Judas witnessed it. When Jesus healed severed spinal cords and optic nerves, Judas watched it happen. Judas shared a million unrecorded moments with Jesus we'll know nothing about.

Seriously, after three years walking side by side with Jesus, couldn't Judas walk one more day with Him to the cross?

Judas played the part, but the truth never pierced his heart. He never embraced Jesus with true faith. But what would motivate Judas to walk into the Sanhedrin's snake pit and offer to spy on Jesus? Maybe he saw the end coming, and wanted out—but not without compensation for three wasted years. He wanted a kingdom, not a cross. He wanted the money. So he gave Satan the foothold to destroy him.

For the whole last week, Judas looked for his moment to set Jesus up—and collect the promised thirty pieces of silver—enough to buy a new wardrobe, or a slave, or a small piece of land.

No one suspected Judas, except of course, Jesus. At their last supper together, He sat Judas in the place of honor, next to Him so they could talk privately. Even knowing what Judas was about to do, Jesus washed his feet. He gave Judas every opportunity to turn around, even at this 11th hour.

"One of you will betray me," Jesus finally announced. Did Judas look up from his plate at Jesus? Did he hesitate going through with his plan? But in that final moment, Satan saw Judas' vulnerability and enters him and Judas' door of opportunity slams shut.

"What you are about to do, do quickly," Jesus whispers to him. The next time we see Judas, he's leading 600 Roman guards right to Jesus—identifying Him with a kiss in a crowd on a dark night.

It's hard to guess why later that night Judas woke to the shameful thing he'd done. He tried to undo his treachery by giving back the money to the ones who had planned the ambush, but they laughed at him.

Satan laughed at Judas, too. He convinced him his life was over. And Judas' body hung from his belt on the southeast side of Jerusalem before morning.

Not far away, Jesus' body was broken for Judas and every sinner like him who will just turn around. *Here's your life back*, it's like Jesus was saying, *By faith, take My forgiveness and live.*

Tomorrow: *One on one with Jesus, a picture of restoration*

 Let's talk about it:

1. Reflect on all that Judas witnessed for himself. Why did it make no difference in his decision to betray Jesus?
2. Satan used Judas' love of money to get a foothold in destroying his life and hurting Jesus. Read Ephesians 4:7. How does our sin give Satan the advantage in our lives?

━━ DAY 13 ━━

Peter

with the One who restores broken people

And Peter remembered the saying of Jesus, "Before the rooster crows, you will deny me three times." And he went out and wept bitterly.
Matthew 26:75

Why did I say that? Why didn't I do something? Be honest, you've asked yourself this, too.

Like the rest of the team, Peter ran when the soldiers arrested Jesus, but he didn't go far. He watched everything unfold from the shadows, keeping an eye on Jesus until He disappeared behind the locked doors of the high priest's palace.

Even then, Peter stayed close. He warmed his hands around a small fire in the courtyard. Perhaps when someone poked the fire and a blaze lit Peter's face, a servant girl called him out. *Hey, you're with that Galilean! I know you!*

That moment in Caiaphas' courtyard marked the greatest crisis of Peter's life. For a lifetime he must have wished he could snatch back his words.

"I don't know Him!" He spit out not once, but three times. Just hours before, he said to Jesus, *I'll die with you, Master! Others will turn away, Lord, but I won't.*

Somewhere in the night, a rooster stretched its neck and announced his failure. Just then, Peter looked over his shoulder and caught the eye of the One who loved him more than life, passing through the courtyard on His way to the cross.

That moment between sinner and Savior hung in the air like a framed picture.

Peter turned away from the fire and wept. What burned more— the smoke in his eyes or the conviction in his heart?

Go ahead and be hard on Peter. Talk about how impulsive he was or how he shot off his mouth. But something changed Peter between the devastating moment by this fire and when he stood with the Lord by another fire a couple mornings later.

In those days in-between, Peter's guilt could have driven him to the cynical edge. (*What was I thinking to believe He was the Christ, anyway?*) He could have run, never to return. Unbelief could have hardened his heart. For sure, if you don't deal with sin, it can drive you to an awful place.

But that's not the Peter we meet three days later rushing into Jesus' empty tomb, or the Peter who throws himself into the lake to get to Jesus, or the Peter who Jesus pulls aside in private conversation and restores to friendship and ministry. Did they speak of that awful moment by the fire? That's between them.

What we do know is Peter's crisis took him to the right place with God. Sin, rightly understood, prompted repentance. And repentance turned him around. Even after he failed, Peter ran back to the Lord with a whole heart, stronger, more humble, ready for God to take him somewhere new.

If you've ever thought, "I've gone too far" . . . let Jesus restore you. You can get up again. Just ask Peter.

Tomorrow: *One on one with Jesus and the cast of players.*

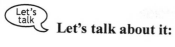 **Let's talk about it:**

1. What are ways you've experienced or seen others deal with guilt?
2. What's so great about repentance?

DAY 14

Unjust

The One who entrusted Himself to God

Then those who had seized Jesus led him to Caiaphas the high priest, where the scribes and the elders had gathered. And Peter was following him at a distance, as far as the courtyard of the high priest, and going inside he sat with the guards to see the end. Matthew 26:57-58

The tabloids would have torn the story apart but only the Jewish priests and Roman police knew what was happening Friday morning between midnight and 8 a.m. Justice turned a blind eye in Jerusalem that day.

Plot: From Gethsemane, a garrison of soldiers led Jesus through empty streets to Annas' house (midnight), then to Caiaphas (1 a.m.), then to the Sanhedrin (early morning), then to Pilate (before 6 a.m.), then to Herod Antipas (7 a.m.), then to Pilate (8 a.m.) then to the Cross (9 a.m.).

Cast of Characters:

Annas: *The master puppeteer.* That Jesus is brought first to Annas, the former High Priest, hints at who ordered the lynch mob. Annas hoped to intimidate Jesus but Jesus wouldn't have it. Verdict: The guards beat Jesus for showing disrespect. Annas sends Jesus to Caiaphas (his son-in-law.)

Caiaphas: *The profiteer.* Jesus threatened the highly lucrative temple business Caiaphas ran with the Sanhedrin and threatened the peace he needed to maintain to keep Rome out of his business. Verdict: Jesus declared guilty of blasphemy.

The Sanhedrin: *Religious dinner theatre.* The court held to try Jesus had more drama than late night. But Jesus on the stand stayed silent until they asked Him, "Are you the Christ, the Son of God?" His answer, "yes," sealed the verdict. Verdict: Jesus declared guilty of blasphemy but sent to Roman court for political treason.

Pilate: *Professional politician.* Pilate had no skin in this game the Jewish leaders waged against the Galilean prophet. His instinct said the accused was innocent. But he couldn't afford the consequences if he didn't play along. Since Herod Antipas, tetrarch over Galilee, was in town for Passover, Pilate sent Jesus to him as an olive branch. Verdict: Jesus declared innocent but sent to Herod Agrippa to judge.

Herod Antipas: *Sly opportunist.* Antipas' father was Herod the Great (the one who killed the babies in the Christmas story). Like father like son, Herod Antipas recently beheaded Jesus' cousin, John the Baptist. Herod, who Jesus once called "the fox" (slamming Herod's masculinity), was glad to finally meet the miracle-worker of Galilee. He commanded his prisoner to do a miracle. You can guess how that turned out. Verdict: Jesus mistreated and mocked; Herod made no decision but sent Jesus back to Pilate.

Pilate: When Jesus came back, cruelly roughed up, Pilate thought of a new way out: release Jesus as the annual Passover-pardoned prisoner. The Sanhedrin overruled him, "Not Jesus—release Barabbas, the murderer." He had Jesus stripped naked, tied to a post and scourged—a technique designed to come just short of killing the strongest man. Pilate presents Jesus to the crowd, hoping now for their mercy. Instead they cry, "Crucify Him." In a thinly veiled threat, the Sanhedrin demand Jesus' death and Pilate sees it's either him or Jesus. "Let Him be crucified then," and Pilate washes his hands of the whole thing. Verdict: Jesus declared innocent but overruled by a mob.

At first light, the curtain rises on the greatest rescue plan since time began. Jesus, aware of these trials' scams, kept entrusting Himself to His Father who judges all things justly. A model for us all in a day when miscarried justice and political trickery are frequent headlines.

Tomorrow: *One on one with Jesus and the truth-seeker*

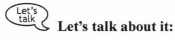

Let's talk about it:

1. What lesson does this teach us about true justice?
2. Have you ever been judged/treated unfairly? How does this illustrate how God uses the miscarriage of justice? Does it give you hope?

238

DAY 15

Pilate

The One who is the truth

Then Pilate said to him, "So you are a king?" Jesus answered, "You say that I am a king. For this purpose I was born and for this purpose I have come into the world—to bear witness to the truth. Everyone who is of the truth listens to my voice." Pilate said to him, "What is truth?"
John 18:37-38

When it was over and two disciples came to ask permission to take down Jesus' body from the cross, a depression descended on Pilate he would never shake.

So He's dead, he thought. *Well, my hands are clean of the whole mess*, he lied to himself. *I wanted no part of this man's death.*

In all his years of playing political chess, this match tripped him up. He had the power to stop an unjust execution—the murder—of an innocent man and he didn't. A deliberate miscarriage of justice. Thinking he was king, Pilate played the pawn to evil itself.

He tried, he reasoned to himself. Three times he said right out, "this man is innocent of any crime." It didn't matter. His opponents,

Herod Antipas and the Sanhedrin, held his neck in the noose with their tattletale reports to Rome and taunted him with threats, "No friend of Caesar's would let Jesus live…"

That's when he finally caved to public opinion. *Let them have their Nazarene,* even when he knew their evil game.

Pilate was no fool. History tells how he won brave battles on the field and in Roman legislature. Tiberius, the king of the world at the time, awarded him the prize of ruling Judea. To be honest, Pilate couldn't stand the conspiring, petty politics of the local religious leaders. Neither could he stomach the morals of the tiny tyrant, Herod Antipas.

But when his own political ambition was on the line, Pilate played fast and easy. Never mind his wife warned him about prosecuting an innocent man. Never mind his uneasy debate with the accused. *What is truth anyway?* Best not be controlled by something you can't understand, he thought.

But you have to wonder if when Pilate sat alone on his balcony each night and replayed the day's drama, he was haunted by his encounter with Jesus. In the end, we all wonder about who we are and who God is and if it's true what they say about heaven and hell. That's the truth he really wanted to know.

You also have to wonder if his question was sincere or sarcastic, "What is truth?" Did he recognize the One who said, "I am the truth," standing right in front of him?

Somehow, Pilate must have known he missed something significant and it may have cost him everything.

Tomorrow: *One on one with Jesus and the shepherd boy grown up*

Let's talk about it:

1. How is Pilate a lot like people you know?
2. Ask God to prompt a conversation for you with someone today who is looking for the truth. Then ask Him for the words to say for Him to stir faith in them.

DAY 16

Shepherd, Part 3

The One who walked through the valley of the shadow

And as they led him away, they seized one Simon of Cyrene, who was coming in from the country, and laid on him the cross, to carry it behind Jesus. And there followed him a great multitude of the people and of women who were mourning and lamenting for him. Luke 23:26-27

I was there when He came into the world and I was there when He left.

A few weeks ago, my grandson and I talked with Rabbi Jesus in the temple court. "You know, David, a good shepherd lays down his life for his sheep." This morning I got word from Jerusalem He was doing just that. I ran the five miles from Bethlehem straight to the old city. Near the Praetorium I heard, "Crucify Him, Crucify Him."

Is that Him? His body, so ripped apart I couldn't be sure. The Roman guard pushed the Rabbi off the ledge. He stumbled, too weak to stand. A blow to His head sent Him to His knees.

"Stop it! Don't you know who He is?" I screamed.

"Get out of here, Sheep Dog" spit the guard. But Jesus lifted His swollen face and looked up at me, "David," He whispered.

They pushed Him inch by inch through the streets, a crossbeam pressing into His back. When He hesitated, they flogged Him more. Women hid their children as He passed. Others spit. Most shuddered at His shredded body.

Finally, Jesus fell and laid still. The soldiers had tortured Him too much. To keep from killing Him before He could be executed, they drug a man from the crowd and shoved the crossbeam onto his back. I rushed in, "please, let me help Him," and they nodded. I took Jesus by the waist, threw His arm around my shoulder and lifted His almost dead weight to His feet.

"Thank you, my friend." His voice hoarse. Step by painful step, we walked. Every breath labored. Every touch painful. Every prophecy about His suffering being fulfilled. He was the lamb to the slaughter.

"How are things in Bethlehem?" Jesus' words, an attempted distraction, lay low and close to my ear.

"Let me tell you about Bethlehem, Rabbi." I held His quivering side. "On the night you were born, we were in the field, my father and uncles and me. When the sky exploded with bright, beautiful angels, the host shouted, 'Glory to God! A Savior has been born to you; He is Mashiach, the Lord.' And we ran over rocks and fields to where we found You with Your mother and Joseph. They looked so young—my age—and so tired and scared."

"They were wonderful parents..."

"Easy now. Let me help you. Throw your weight on me." My face beside His, I smelled a strong oil in His hair. I knew it. Myrrh—burial oil. My eyes burned with the strong scent mixed with our sweat.

"You're a good shepherd, David."

"Yes, Lord, I learned it from you. *The Lord is my shepherd. I want no other.*"

He continued, *"He makes me lie...down in...green pastures...He leads me beside...still waters."*

242

"He restores my soul."

"When I walk through . . . the valley of the shadow . . . .. of death, I will fear no . . . evil." We turned the corner outside the gate and saw the prepared posts in the Place of the Skull. The soldiers waiting. Jesus moaned from deep within.

"The Father will give you the strength, Jesus. Focus on the horizon, what's ahead. You're going home. And the angels will sing and shout again like they did for You in Bethlehem."

"I just want to finish. I want to save. You'll stay?"

"Yes, I'll stay." And with that, the guards threw us apart and Jesus crumbled in the dirt. They swarmed Him with shouts and spikes and when they drove the nails into Him, His cry pierced my soul.

I stood there in His line of vision all morning. After noon when the darkness covered everything, I didn't leave Him. No, not until they took His body down before the Sabbat trumpet sounded did I move. Now, I walk home under the stars, my heart both full and grieving. I was with Him at His birth and now with Him in His death. I know exactly who He is. He is Messiah, Savior of the world.

Note: This is an imaginative rendering of Jesus' walk to the Cross, but the lessons are true. When you can, walk with people in their suffering. In their moments of highest vulnerability let them hear God's Word and as you share it, invite God's Spirit to comfort them. Key passages are Psalm 23, Romans 8:16-17, John 14:1-4.

Tomorrow: *One on one with Jesus and the one who should have died*

Let's talk about it:

1. How does this fictional story of David in all three seasons of His life, help to make Jesus' story personal?
2. Would you have liked to help Jesus on the day He died?

DAY 17

Barabbas

The One who died in my place

But the chief priests stirred up the crowd to have him release for them Barabbas instead. And Pilate again said to them, "Then what shall I do with the man you call the King of the Jews?" And they cried out again, "Crucify him." And Pilate said to them, "Why? What evil has he done?" But they shouted all the more, "Crucify him." So Pilate, wishing to satisfy the crowd, released for them Barabbas, and having scourged Jesus, he delivered him to be crucified. Mark 15:11-15

Fear takes over when you're alone on death row and hear the crowds outside shout your name. Then a second later, you hear them demand, "Crucify him."

You have nothing left to handle the terror. Of course, you know you're guilty and it terrifies you out of your mind. I am Barabbas, the notorious revolutionary, the militant robber and murderer.

Now the guards come for me. The steady cadence of their march down the hall, louder, louder, till they stop at my cell, and with it, my heart stops, too. Their keys wrangle the lock and the door screams open on its hinges. One last look around the cell, in a cold sweat I drop into their ranks. They pull my shackled wrists down the hall; I pass another prisoner being led to my cell. Our eyes meet for a split second. His barely open, the blood trail down His face and bits of flesh torn from His skull. But in that split second, I see . . . what? I've never seen that before.

He's thrown into my cell and the door slams shut. But I'm led out the entrance and into the light. Squinting against the bright sunshine, I'm pushed into the crowd who had screamed my name. Now they break into a cheer. The guard unshackles my wrists, and spits, "Released."

Pilate from the podium, "Here is your choice: Barabbas, the rebel murderer." And under his breath, "May whatever God who lives have mercy on your souls."

The people, worked up in a frenzy by crooked religious leaders with a vendetta, exchanged Jesus, the innocent, for Barabbas, the guilty. Given the same choice, Jesus would have spared Barabbas, too. For He came to die for sinners and Barabbas qualified.

Barabbas is the first person who can say, "Jesus died for my sins." Literally, Jesus changed places with him. The middle cross was meant for Barabbas, in between two of his mercenary sidekicks. Jesus took the punishment the rebel deserved while Barabbas walked out free.

There's no better picture of what happens to us, too, when we accept Jesus as our substitute.

We don't know much about Barabbas but perhaps that's by design. We can just as easily write our own sins on the sign above Jesus' head. Guilty.

And who knows but in the dark hours later that day when Barabbas hung on the fringes of the crowd and watched his two friends, and the One he passed in the hallway, hang from their crosses. He couldn't look away. Hardly recognizable in His tortured

245

body, there was Jesus, dying on the middle cross and yet he walks free.

And so is every sinner who recognizes the mercy of that moment when Jesus died in their place. In your place. Jesus, your substitute.

Tomorrow: *One on one with Jesus on the cross*

 Let's talk about it:

1. Mercy—not getting what you deserve. Do you think differently about Barabbas once you understand how God gave him mercy?
2. Here's an easy way to summarize the gospel. Which one works for you?
   The gospel in four words: Jesus took my place.
   The gospel in three words: Him for me.
   The gospel in two words: substitutionary atonement
   The gospel in one word: Jesus

DAY 18

Mary and John at the Cross

The One who is our life

But standing by the cross of Jesus were his mother and his mother's sister, Mary the wife of Clopas, and Mary Magdalene. When Jesus saw his mother and the disciple whom he loved standing nearby, he said to his mother, "Woman, behold, your son!" Then he said to the disciple, "Behold, your mother!" And from that hour the disciple took her to his own home.
John 19:25-27

Did it have to be like this? That's what I thought as we stood there with Him," Mary said. "It was the most painful, confusing, profound moment of my life."

John nodded. He had no words at the memory. Even now, eleven years later, he grieved again those hours he stood with Mary and watched Jesus die.

The fresh news that James has now been murdered—beheaded like John the Baptist—flooded John with grief. It was 44 A.D. Ephesus. Far from Jerusalem. Far from the cross, yet in a heartbeat, John was back there. Recently, he brought Mary to Turkey to escape

Herod Agrippa's death-grip on Galilee. They got out just in time. His brother did not.

James, the other "son of thunder," would be the first of their group to die for the Lord. *James would be fine with that*, John smirked. If tonight his brother sat across from him, he would be the first to volunteer to die. Peter would fight him for the privilege. And what's this other news from home? Peter rescued from death row by an angel? Of course, he was. (Laughing)

But in the bittersweet memories, John's spirit struggled. It was death, after all. First, his Lord. Now, his brother.

Never had John seen death like at Jesus' cross. Tortured in spirit and body, Jesus' flesh turned inside out. So grisly John feared he would vomit on the spot. He just focused on Jesus' face and kept eye-contact with Him as much as he could. And he looked after his aunt, Mary.

So, this is the sword, she had said. "I'd worried for years what the old man in the temple meant. But when I stood there, I knew," Mary's fist bounced off the table. " . . I didn't know how to pray, you know? I begged for the life of my innocent son. But I knew somehow—really since Gabriel told me about Him—that it would be this way. Didn't Isaiah the prophet say Messiah would suffer? I just wanted it to be different."

"Still—in all His agony, He thought of you," John touched Mary's arm.

"Dear woman, here is your son," she whispered.

"And here is your mother," John finished. "A gift to us both." They sat in the quiet. "Did you have any time with Him when He returned?"

"Yes, brief, just the two of us. It was after we all left Jerusalem. He showed up one Sabbat back in our old house in Galilee. All the family was gathered for dinner. I was out back getting vegetables from storage. I turned around with my peppers and tomatoes and there He was, sitting in His favorite spot on the wall. Just like the million times we sat back there and talked."

"What did you say to Him?"

"At first I had no words, I could only cry and laugh and hug Him. I looked at His scars, I told Him I was sorry for trying to keep Him from Jerusalem. I knew He was about His Father's business; He always was. I was just selfish, just being a mother, wanting Him near me . . . I thanked Him, too. I'm still trying to understand it but, He died for me that day, too, to pay for my sin, as He said. He came to save me, too.

"I was the first to love Him, John, but He loved me even before that. I was the first to hear His words. I was the first to share His suffering. All those years, no one except Joseph and I knew who He was. And then when Joseph was gone, only me.

"I had Him all to myself for a little bit. Of all people, I knew He was so much more than we knew. Everything I've learned since confirms it. When I think of that horrible day in Jerusalem, I see God's Son and my son, my Savior . . . and my Lord. He is my life, John."

"You were His first disciple," John smiled.

"Yes, I guess I was." Then quickly, "He liked oranges. When we sat out back, He'd pick one off the tree and we'd share it and talk. I smile even now when I smell oranges."

Tomorrow: *One on one with Jesus and a new look at the cross.*

 Let's talk about it:

1. Is it curious to you to think of the "normalcy" of Jesus' life and relationships? ("He liked oranges...") What would you like to ask Him?

2. From the perspective of time, how do you see significant events from your life differently? Perhaps when you first came to Jesus as Savior or the early days of walking with Him?

DAY 19

The Cross

The One who reminds us of the cross

I have been crucified with Christ. It is no longer I who live, but Christ who lives in me. And the life I now live in the flesh I live by faith in the Son of God, who loved me and gave himself for me. Galatians 2:20

When the unthinkable becomes reality, it takes the perspective of another world to make it beautiful. That's the cross. On our soil, it speaks of injustice, suffering—a good life cut short. But to you who believe, who are learning to breath another air, the cross is precious because of what it means. The impact of the cross is layered and nuanced and will take a million years or more to understand but we can begin here and now. Ask the Lord to show you.

What does Your cross mean to me?

1. If Your cross is comfortable for me, easy to wear around my neck, hang on my walls or from my neck, remind me of its offense.
2. Every time I take my sin lightly, remind me what it cost You.
3. Every time I carry my own burden, remind me that Your cross is my rescue.
4. When I struggle with a wrong that needs righted, or a loss to be redeemed, remind me how Your cross bridges the gap.
5. When today isn't enough to satisfy this eternity in my heart, remind me what Your cross promises.
6. If I refuse to accept Your forgiveness and carry my guilt instead, remind me why the cross was the only way to God.
7. If I fear I've gone too far to be saved and doubt if you can keep me saved, remind me of the safety of Your cross.
8. In case the horrors of Calvary overwhelm me, remind me of Your joy in the cross.
9. Someday when I stand forgiven, complete, and accepted before God, I will remember Your cross for its beauty.
10. And on that day when every knee bows and every tongue confesses You are Lord, Jesus, I won't hide my eyes from Your scars.

Tomorrow: *One on one with Jesus, the One who died in my place*

 Let's talk about it:

1. Which statement above made you pause and think about personally?
2. "What does the cross mean to me?" Ask God to help you think that out. Write down your thoughts, perhaps in your journal or the back of your Bible. Return to it often.

DAY 20

The Thief

& the One who invites you home

One of the criminals who were hanged railed at him, saying, "Are you not the Christ? Save yourself and us!" But the other rebuked him, saying, "Do you not fear God, since you are under the same sentence of condemnation? And we indeed justly, for we are receiving the due reward of our deeds; but this man has done nothing wrong." And he said, "Jesus, remember me when you come into your kingdom." ⁴³ And he said to him, "Truly, I say to you, today you will be with me in paradise." Luke 23:32-43

The thief on the third cross next to Jesus is every one of us. **Every one of us is surprised by how life turns.**

The only thing we know about this thief is he was a hardened criminal. Let's call him Sam. Maybe not hardened from the start, but one bad decision led to another and even Sam admitted he deserved to be there. Likely all three crosses were reserved for Barabbas' crew, only instead of their leader hanging on the middle cross, instead they pinned a country rabbi to the sky.

Every one of us has a secret something that keeps us from God.

It could be as obvious as Sam's crime or as subtle as something only you know you did. In your heart, you know you're far from God. You may work hard at being good and doing good, but nothing spans the distance. And so you make-do. You rationalize, hide, hurl—anything to keep from feeling the distance.

Sam and his notorious partner mocked Jesus at first. But something changed as they suffered. One grew more bitter. And one hung on every word Jesus said. "Father, forgive them," Sam heard Jesus whisper in measured, pained breaths.

"Forgive them? Jesus, forgive me!"

Everyone knew Jesus was a famous teacher, but Sam would never ask a teacher for forgiveness. From his weird, surreal vantage point, Sam realized Jesus was more. He was a Savior, in the process of saving.

Every one of us has enough information about Jesus to decide.

Life drained from them all, hanging there. The first thief hung on to pride. But Sam humbled himself. With the courage of the desperate, he reached out to the middle cross and asked, "Jesus, remember me when You come into Your kingdom." That's all he could say. It was his last prayer, and maybe his first. He said it with faith and it turned out to be enough.

Jesus wasn't dying for people who deserved mercy. His last intentional act, at His most wounded, was to save one more person who didn't deserve it. That one could have been you.

Every one of us can be welcomed into Jesus' presence.

"Today you will be with Me in paradise," Jesus assured the man next to Him. No one in history ever died with such certainty of immediate grace. Yet every one of us gets the same invitation. No one needs to suffer for eternity without Jesus. No one needs to die alone.

When the soldiers broke his legs and he could no longer push himself up to breathe, Sam let go of the end of the rope and dropped into eternity and safely into Jesus' arms. And that's where he still is today.

Tomorrow: *One on one with Jesus, the forgiver*

 Let's talk about it:

1. Which of the four statements above do you most resonate with?
2. How is Sam like someone you know? Like you?

DAY 21

Forgiveness

The One who bought the gift

but God shows his love for us in that while we were still sinners, Christ died for us. Since, therefore, we have now been justified by his blood, much more shall we be saved by him from the wrath of God. Romans 5:8-9

The first thing Jesus prayed from the cross described in a nutshell why He hung there in the first place. "Father forgive them . . ." — forgive those who tortured and took His life. Forgive those who live apart from You, who miss the mark in any way . . .

Without forgiveness, Jesus' murder is just another tragic story. Another good man sacrificed by a frenzied crowd. Another biography that doesn't get a happily ever after.

That's what our story would be if Jesus didn't pay for our sins and ask God to apply that mercy to our account.

Believe the truth about forgiveness.

Without forgiveness, we're numb to the depth and gravity of our destiny before a God so holy even love can't span the distance between us.

"So I'm not perfect; who is?"

Only Jesus. Only He could pay for sin. Only He didn't owe a dime. Only He can get you out of jail for what you think could never be forgiven.

Some think they can have a relationship with God without His forgiveness. They try hard to hide, dismiss, or work off their guilt. They try to forgive themselves. The same is true about shame. But the debt is too big, the gap between you and God, too wide.

Forgiveness says, "let Jesus carry your guilt. Let Him take the shame." Your only option is Jesus. Only His death can span the distance. All that we've studied about His healing and teaching find their meaning in this moment: He came to rescue you through the forgiveness found on the cross.

Stop admiring forgiveness at a distance. Come in from the fringes. Stop thinking, "Yes, Jesus, forgive *them* . . . someone *else* for something *else*. Not me. Not my stuff. I don't need it. Or my thing is too awful." Resist the impulse to run, to escape pain rather than confront it. To carry the guilt rather than surrender it.

Lay that defensiveness down and come join the community of the broken.

While you were the worst you can be, Jesus died for you. Love and grace meet at the cross and forgiveness flows from Jesus' brokenness to yours. You become whole for the first time.

Forgiveness is like a gift from someone who knows you really well—the perfect gift you really need but could never afford to get for yourself. Even before you knew you needed it, Jesus bought it for you.

Want to receive it? Begin here: *Jesus, thank You for dying in my place. Thank You for paying a debt You didn't owe, for me, who owes a debt I cannot pay . . .*

Tomorrow: *One on one with Jesus on the cross*

Let's talk about it:

1. "Believe the truth about forgiveness." What lies have you believed about God's forgiveness? What is the truth?
2. How have you tried to pay your own debt? What does the truth about forgiveness mean to you now?

DAY 22

Finished

The One who carries your sin

After this, Jesus, knowing that all was now finished, said (to fulfill the Scripture), "I thirst." A jar full of sour wine stood there, so they put a sponge full of the sour wine on a hyssop branch and held it to his mouth. When Jesus had received the sour wine, he said, "It is finished," and he bowed his head and gave up his spirit. John 19:28-30

He's the marathon runner breaking the tape.

A firefighter emerging from the smoke.

A soldier limping home.

Jesus pulled Himself up on the nails. With everything left in Him, He shouts, "IT IS FINISHED."

For us, three powerful words—in the Greek, just one: *TETELESTAI.* People standing near the cross heard Him say it, and knew exactly what Jesus meant.

Complete. Paid in full. Done.

Tetelestai belonged to the Day of Atonement. Yom Kippur is the most important day on the Jewish calendar. For one day, they absolutely knew their sin was paid for. Momentarily.

On this day under Old Testament law, two goats were taken to the Temple. One—sacrificed, and its blood sprinkled on the mercy seat in the Holy of Holies symbolizing the shed blood that paid the price for sin. On the other goat, the high priest laid his hands and confessed the sins of the people. It now symbolically carried all their sins. They, then drove this "scapegoat" outside the city walls and far into the wilderness, symbolizing their guilt being taken far away.

Along the way out of the city, other priests were stationed and they called back to the temple when the scapegoat had been successfully driven away, perhaps over a cliff, so the guilt could not return. From one post to the next, one priest shouted the message back, "It is finished. It is finished." The message, *tetelestrai*, resonated all the way back to the city until the temple priest announced to the people that their sins had been paid in full. They were good for another year.

When Jesus shouted, "It is finished," every Jew standing around the cross recognized it.

It is finished. Your sins have been carried far away. They are forgiven.

It is finished. No more animals need to be sacrificed. No more does the river of blood need to flow out of the Temple.

It is finished. The price has been paid in full.

All that remains is what you decide to do with what Jesus did for you. Somebody must pay. Do you carry your own sin, or will you let Him carry it for you?

Consider Jesus on the cross:

- He is our great High Priest. Read Hebrews 4:14.
- He is the "Lamb that was slain from the creation of the world." Revelation 13:8
- He is our scapegoat. His blood paid sin's price. 2 Cor 5:21, Hebrews 10:3-4, 10
- Your sin was laid on Him. Isaiah 53:6

You can carry your sin yourself—or accept His offer to carry it for you. Your choice.

Tomorrow: *One on one with Jesus on the cross*

 Let's talk about it:

1. Read Hebrews 4:14-16. How does this impact how you pray?
2. Read Isaiah 53:6 and Revelation 13:8. What does this picture of Jesus mean to you?

DAY 23

Lullaby

The One who keeps your soul safe

Then Jesus, calling out with a loud voice, said, "Father, into your hands I commit my spirit!" And having said this he breathed his last. Luke 23:46

Now I lay me down to sleep, I pray the Lord my soul to keep . . . Moms and dads in every generation have prayed with their little ones before bedtime, assuring them that they were safe while they slept.

Like a bedtime lullaby, Jewish parents also taught their little ones to entrust their soul to God for safekeeping until morning. They taught them to pray Psalm 31:5, "Into Your hands I commit my spirit."

"Commit my spirit" means to "deposit" it—like you deposit money in a bank account. You hand it over for safekeeping, fully intending to get it back.

Every night as He fell asleep, Jesus most likely prayed, "into Your hands I commit my spirit." He learned it as a boy from Mary

261

and Joseph. The pattern of His life was to pray this at night and in the morning thank God for keeping His soul safe.

Now here as He faced the greatest challenge of His earthly life, Jesus prayed it again with His last ounce of strength. In the horror of dying, Jesus was likely reciting to Himself the first verses of Psalm 31:

For you, O LORD, are my rock and my fortress; and for your name's sake you lead me and guide me; you take me out of the net they have hidden for me, for you are my refuge.

(And then He cried aloud) ***Into your hand I commit my spirit; you have redeemed me, O LORD, faithful God.***

By faith, Jesus deposited His soul into His Father's hands, knowing He would get it back again when His life was returned to Him.

In the cross' final moments, Jesus knew He had now paid in full the debt of sin. God the Father's holiness was satisfied and the chasm between them was bridged.

Jesus called Him *Father* again. It was a tender moment between a loving daddy and a dying son as the Son of God laid His life down.

Tomorrow: *One on one with the One who died in your place.*

 Let's talk about it:

1. Tonight, as you turn out the lights before sleep, pray like Jesus did, "Father, into Your hands I commit my spirit." Then thank Him in the morning that He kept your soul safe.
2. Read Psalm 31. What comfort does this offer someone afraid or anxious?

DAY 24

Victory

The One who won the war

But thanks be to God, who in Christ always leads us in triumphal procession, and through us spreads the fragrance of the knowledge of him everywhere. For we are the aroma of Christ to God among those who are being saved and among those who are perishing, 2 Corinthians 2:14-15

No one wants to live a meaningless life—or die a useless death. Including Jesus. He lived every day on purpose and died the same way.

The Bible tells us Jesus' purpose was to "to save His people from their sins" (Matthew 1:21) and to "destroy the devil's work (1 John 3:8). No wonder Satan tried every possible way to keep Jesus off his playground and keep Him from saving us. And if he couldn't do that, then at least he'd try to steal every bit of joy along the way.

Satan didn't want Jesus crucified, he just wanted Him dead.

- Remember King Herod's savage massacre of all the baby boys in Bethlehem? That was Satan at work.

263

- Remember a couple times along the way when crowds picked up rocks to stone Jesus? That was Satan stoking the frenzy.
- Remember Jesus' internal agony, His bloody sweat, in Gethsemane? Satan was likely behind that, too.

Satan did anything he could to keep Jesus from fulfilling His two-fold purpose: to die for us and to destroy him.

Sometimes Satan was tricky. Remember when he tempted Jesus in the wilderness? He smoothly reasoned, "You shouldn't have to die . . . use Your power to escape suffering. If you're the Son of God, show Your right to reign. I can help you do it." If Jesus bought that lie, He couldn't be our Savior.

When Jesus wouldn't listen to Satan, the enemy thought perhaps Jesus would listen to one of His men . . . Remember when Peter first heard Jesus say He was going to Jerusalem to die? Peter said, "never, Lord!" And Jesus said, "Get behind me, Satan!" Jesus recognized Satan's strategy even when it came through someone He loved.

Satan used another of Jesus' men, Judas, to turn on Him. Far from innocent, Judas loved money and that gave Satan the foothold he needed to use Judas to make Jesus suffer more. If he couldn't keep Jesus from the cross, at least he could make it as painful as possible.

But in every attack, Jesus kept His focus. He lived and died on purpose.

Satan's attacks continue to this day. He wants nothing more than to hurt Jesus and doesn't mind destroying you in the process.

A very real spiritual war began in your life the day you surrendered your life to Jesus. Your heart became a battlefield. If he can pull you back into your old ways again, well, your destruction is just collateral damage—it's Jesus he's after.

But if you belong to Jesus then He won the war for your life on the cross. He disarmed Satan of every weapon, He broke Satan's stranglehold on your life. At the cross, Jesus won the victory that set you free. That is the truth—call anything else a lie from hell.

Tomorrow: *One on one with Jesus and the centurion*

Let's talk about it:

1. Think about some of your hardest, most private struggles, you've faced since surrendering your life to Jesus Christ. Consider how God has protected you from Satan's schemes.

2. As you face temptation to sin, remember how your sin affects Jesus. "If he can pull you back into your old ways again, well, your destruction is just collateral damage—it's Jesus he's after." Your thoughts?

DAY 25

Centurion

& the One who shook the earth

Then Jesus, calling out with a loud voice, said, "Father, into your hands I commit my spirit!" And having said this he breathed his last. [47] Now when the centurion saw what had taken place, he praised God, saying, "Certainly this man was innocent!" Luke 23:46-47

Excuse me? Jerusalem Tribune here. Are you the captain of the guard? May I ask you a few questions?

Yes, but you'll need to step out of the way.

Oh, of course. First, can you tell us your name and what happened here today?

My name isn't for print, but I am the commander. What happened here is just what you think. An execution of three criminals—No, two criminals and one rabbi from the countryside.

A rabbi—isn't that unusual?

The whole day is unusual. First, they switched the criminals on us. Barabbas was supposed to die, you know, the leader of the insurrection—and with him the other two prisoners. Last night we were preparing the beams for the execution and at midnight, they ordered me to go get a rabbi, Jesus of Nazareth, from Gethsemane. Crazy!—100 of the finest soldiers in the land escorting a peaceful teacher through empty streets. I don't pretend to understand these Jews. But my job is to keep the peace.

Did the execution go as planned?

I suppose so. My men had a bit of sport with the rabbi. The Chief Priests said 'have some fun,' with Him. Like I said, none of it makes sense. But anything to lift the tension is fine by me. My soldiers live with death every day and it gets to you, you know?

They stripped the rabbi and put Him in a cheap robe and made this...this twisted crown of branches and shoved it on His head. They were just playing. Bowing down in front of Him, pretending He was king. He was so beat up, He could barely stand.

But the funny thing, well, not so funny I guess, is that He didn't resist. And the only time He said anything, other than crying out in pain, was when they impaled His wrists. He looked at my sergeant and kind of prayed with His eyes open. "Father, forgive them. They don't know what they do..." My sergeant told me this after they dropped the rabbi's pole in place. The rabbi's kindness spooked him.

I've watched many men die. I don't feel it anymore. But no one died like this rabbi. His eyes bloodied and swollen looked ahead, focused, like there was nothing between Him and the horizon. Sometimes His head snapped back and He talked to the sky, then at the people at His feet—His mother and brother, I think.

When He spoke, it was quiet to them, moving from face to face as if He had a word for them each. Then to the criminal next to Him. Comforting *them*. In the end, He screamed, *"TETELESTAI"*—not in pain, but like His team won at the colosseum. A victory cry— *Finished*! In the end He mumbled something to the sky, and His head dropped to His chest... I heard the death rattle. We ran a spear through Him to be sure.

At that exact moment, I tripped and fell as the ground shook and a loud ripping came from the Mount and the sun just... blew out— like that (snap). It was pure chaos. People screaming, running—in the dark! I called my troops in line and we tried to get order, but I tell you, it was terrifying. Eerie. *Was this the end of the world?* A chilly wind blew through the darkness the exact moment the rabbi died. That was no coincidence. He was no peasant king. This was a righteous man. They were messing with another world when they killed Him. God have mercy.

I don't care what they say—This One, He was different. He was the Son of God. You can print *that* if you want.

Tomorrow: *One on one with Jesus and two brave disciples*

 Let's talk about it:

1. The Centurion's brief testimony speaks to the power of a silent witness. What do you hope people observing you think of Jesus?
2. Let's hope this account of the Centurion's faith was just the beginning of his life in God. As you meet people today, consider where they each are in their spiritual journey—encourage them on, whether they are new in their faith or growing deeper.

DAY 26

Honor

The One they loved

After these things Joseph of Arimathea, who was a disciple of Jesus, but secretly for fear of the Jews, asked Pilate that he might take away the body of Jesus, and Pilate gave him permission. So he came and took away his body. Nicodemus also, who earlier had come to Jesus by night, came bringing a mixture of myrrh and aloes, about seventy-five pounds in weight. So they took the body of Jesus and bound it in linen cloths with the spices, as is the burial custom of the Jews. John 19:38-40

Likely Nicodemus worshipped in the Temple that morning they crucified Jesus. The Sanhedrin intentionally excluded him from their illegal, midnight trial so Nicodemus might have been unaware of what was happening outside the city gate.

Like an eerie omen at high noon, a shadow moved over the Temple Mount. He ran outside with thousands of others to watch the sun eclipse, leaving their world terrified and in total darkness. A cold wind blew through Nicodemus' bones, *Something bad is happening.* And it was, on the other side of the wall.

When he got word of the unholy execution, Nicodemus also heard Jesus was dying alone. "It's time to step forward," he thought. He sought first the Kingdom and they were killing the King, the Messiah he had come to believe. Previously unwilling to risk the consequences of a public faith in Jesus, but ironically now, conviction rose in Nicodemus' spirit. He must stand with Jesus. He would get the help of Joseph of Arimathea, a rich member of the ruling council and also a kingdom-seeker and secret follower of the Nazarene.

Courage isn't always wasted on the young. No one dares to bury the body of an outcast—no one except family. That's the role Joseph and Nicodemus stepped out of the shadows to do. They risked being Jesus' family and performing a task no one else would do. These two grand old men of Jerusalem, true seekers of righteousness, lived their finest hour.

In a gutsy move in a day of witch-hunts, Joseph asked Pilate, who sent Jesus to His cross, for permission to bury Jesus. ("He's dead already?" Pilate sighed.) Urgency drove Joseph's nerve—if they didn't bury Jesus by sundown, His body would hang on the cross the whole weekend, food for vultures. *Please, a little decency.*

Nicodemus gathered the supplies—a cart, a ladder, an eight-foot linen shroud to wrap Jesus' body, and burial spices. He bought 75 pounds—the traditional amount to bury a king. In his generosity, he affirmed Jesus as "King of the Jews"—what Pilate had scribbled on the sign above Jesus' head. Joseph offered his tomb—a brand new site and right around the corner from Golgotha.

Golgotha was nearly deserted when they arrived. Soldiers, a shepherd, a few women lingered in the eerie light after the eclipse but before sunset. The two seniors struggled with the ladder against the crossbeam. Inch by inch, they lowered Him off the wretched instrument. Jesus' vital signs were obvious. His heart, stopped; His brain, stopped. His body, cooled. His skin, greyed. Death's cruel hour had its temporary win but they forbid themselves any grief till they got this job done.

In Joseph's tomb nearby, their clumsy aristocratic hands fumbled to wash the slaughter from Jesus' body and wrap the shroud around His corpse. Tenderly they honored His naked, torn frame with their best efforts. More would need to be done later.

It wasn't until Joseph kicked the wedge away from the circular stone and rolled it into place that the two new, faithful followers caved into sorrow.

The Light of Israel had gone out. But strangely, their new faith shone brighter. When confronted with the choice between fear of God vs. fear of man, they chose wisely. Love conquers fear every time.

Tomorrow: *One on one with Jesus in Jerusalem*

 Let's talk about it:

1. How do you know when the time is right to take a stand for Jesus?
2. This is a tender story of two unexpected disciples. Describe a time you witnessed or heard about a show of faith from an unexpected source. When have you surprised yourself?

DAY 27

Life

The One who beat death

He himself bore our sins in his body on the tree, that we might die to sin and live to righteousness. By his wounds you have been healed. For you were straying like sheep, but have now returned to the Shepherd and Overseer of your souls.
1 Peter 2:24-25

Even without that weekend, Jerusalem is an incredible place.

Three continents meet here. Three faiths claim their beginnings through Father Abraham. Ancient and recent skirmishes scar the landscape. The ible's entire story revolves around this land, and especially Jerusalem. History began and will be completed here.

Yet one event in April two thousand years ago overshadows all others. That was the weekend Jesus Christ suffered, died, and rose again according to the Scriptures.

Jerusalem will always be a holy city to every person whose faith turns them to God. Here's why: If Jesus is your Savior, then it was in Jerusalem your life was set apart. Bought back. Begun. Your life begins at the cross.

It's a paradox, really. History's darkest day became its brightest. The injustices that pinned Jesus to the tree strangely satisfied God's justice.

We try every way in the world to make the cross glamorous, but it can't be done. It was the ancient electric chair, the hangman's noose. Nothing about it was beautiful. It was death in its gore. Undeserved. Sacrificial. The most hideous, blatant injustice in history.

Yet nothing pictures God's love for you more passionately than when Jesus died on that cross. Nothing. And while God the Father gave His love—Jesus, God's Son, gave His life.

Picture it. *The place of the skull is pitch dark though it was only three in the afternoon. Light Himself turned away from His Son as He bore the sins of every person who ever lived. And there Jesus hung, not a soul realizing it was the most epic moment in history.*

Hebrews 12:2 says Jesus thought of you at Calvary, "who for the joy set before Him endured the cross." In the horror of those hours, Jesus focused on the ultimate joy, of presenting you and everyone else who will believe, to His Father. He could have said something like this, "I bought them back, Father; here they are. Love them as You love Me."

Jesus couldn't bear to think of eternity without you, so He endured it—with joy.

And because He died, you can live forever. His resurrection told us His offer was accepted by God—the salvation message plain and simple. No church needs to be built over it to make it sacred. No special language or merit gives you access to God. God invites you to come to Him on the basis of His Son Jesus' death on your behalf. That's all that's necessary.

Here it is from God's Word. Read it carefully:

"He personally bore our sins in his own body on the cross, so that we might be dead to sin and be alive to all that is good. It was the suffering that he bore which has healed you." 1 Peter 2:21-24 (PHILLIPS)

"The preaching of the cross is nonsense to those who are involved in this dying world, but to us who are being saved from

that death it is nothing less than the power of God." 1 Corinthians 1:18 (PHILLIPS)

Tomorrow: One on one with Jesus on the day in-between

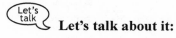 **Let's talk about it:**

1. What is the most personal, most obvious picture of Jesus' love for you? Describe it.
2. Re-read 1 Peter 2:21-24 and 1 Corinthians 1:18. Describe what the cross of Jesus means to you.

═══ DAY 28 ═══

Saturday

The One who is with you in your pain

And we know that for those who love God all things work together for good, for those who are called according to his purpose. Romans 8:28

Most of us live on Easter Saturday. Something tragic or sad happened yesterday and we cling to a promise that all will be made right tomorrow. But we live in today, in between the pain and the hope.

On that first Easter Saturday, on a day designated for Sabbath rest, Jesus' disciples likely had none.

Again, the rooster crowed, waking the day. Semi-conscious, Peter thought, *was it all a nightmare?* But the lingering scent of a charcoal fire hung on his clothes and his eyes burned with regret.

The women were antsy to get back to Jesus' tomb and properly care for His body. In their minds they planned how they would lay Him to rest at tomorrow's first light. They felt restless until they could serve Him this final time.

Without Jesus, the rugged fishermen-turned-disciples likely felt displaced and deserted by their teacher. They sat together in the upper room, each isolated in their private grief. Lonely in this first morning without Jesus. Some imagined they would be next to die. Some wished they could.

And then there were the questions... *How could Jesus have been the long-awaited Messiah if He was just killed? What should we do now? Where was Judas? Was it true that he too was dead?—but by his own hand?*

And the question for all of us, ***how do I live on Easter Saturday?*** After the heartache but before the peace. After the funeral. The trial. The loss. After what you hoped would never happen, just did. How do you live then?

At some point in our lives we all will own this kind of in-between pain. It looks different for each of us, but in the end, pain is pain. What we invested our time, energy, and resources in is gone. Any restoration seems like a far-off dream, at best.

If you are in this in-between place today, here are some truths to help you believe.

- God is with you in this straight place. You're not alone, even if this is how you feel. He's not going to leave you (Hebrews 13:5). Draw near to God and He will draw near to you. He takes special care of the broken-hearted (Psalm 34:18).
- He is working a bigger plan (1 Corinthians 2:9) and will redeem this situation for good (Romans 8:28). Cooperate and He'll work in you a grace and mercy uniquely yours for this season. Believe He's building faith in you—to understand life beyond what you can see (Hebrews 11:1). Emotions aside, believe what's real about God in this moment.
- And surprisingly, a secular someone says it well: "Everything will be okay in the end. If it's not okay, it's not the end." Walk with God *through* this difficult season and He will give your life purpose and meaning both in this moment and on the other side of it.

276

You might be living on Easter Saturday today, but be sure, Sunday is coming.

Believe God is with you, He's writing a bigger story, and if you trust Him today, you will smile again tomorrow—and maybe even laugh when you get a good look at the whole story.

Tomorrow: *One on one with Jesus at daybreak*

 Let's talk about it:

1. Do you ever feel like you're living on Easter Saturday? Describe "the middle" as you experience it.
2. What questions do people have on Easter Saturday? How can you point them towards perseverance and faith? Encourage each other with Hebrews 12:1-3.

DAY 29

Good News

The One who came back for us

If Christ has not been raised, your faith is futile and you are still in your sins. 1 Corinthians 15:17

Jesus is alive.

When Peter heard the news—or just the hint of it, he couldn't get to the tomb fast enough . . . *What if it's true?* Three days of sorrow, inertia, and rehearsing his failure—he was good and ready for hope. That's the difference between Peter and Judas. Both needed forgiveness, Peter humbled himself to go get it.

When the Centurion heard the news, something in him wasn't surprised. Yes, he witnessed Jesus' death. He heard Him cry "Eloi, Eloi." He saw His head drop, His eyes unseeing, His body grey. But the way the rabbi died convinced him He was no ordinary man. Even the rocks shook at the injustice. The sun hid. If Jesus was alive, he had to go find Him.

When Joseph of Arimathea and Nicodemus heard the news, they traded their shock and surprise with a smile at first, then maybe full on laughter. Of all people, they knew what death looked like last Friday afternoon. In days since, their maverick move to care for Jesus upended their identity, power, and comfort with the council, but they regretted nothing. Now this amazing news proved it all worth it.

When Pilate heard the news, he cursed the political hotbed of this backwater region. *He knew this situation would bite him somehow. So much for truth . . .*

When Satan's demons heard the news, ungodly groans echoed in shockwaves through the satanic realm. This was God's checkmate in their game of thrones. Jesus defeated their cruel master. Their doom is now just a matter of time.

If you could hear the news again for the first time, what would you think? Surreal? Epic? Wonderful? Everything about your life in God hangs on this one truth: Jesus suffered and died for your sins, then God raised Him to new life. If Jesus did not rise from the dead, 1 Corinthians 15:17 says our faith means nothing and we're still prisoners of our sins.

But because Jesus rose from the dead, you can say:

- Sin no longer has a hold on me. I am forgiven. Set free. Paid up. Clean before God.
- My faith has a resting place. It doesn't float around to anything sounding spiritual—it's anchored in Jesus, in His sacrificial death for me and His resurrection, proving the debt was paid; the mission was accomplished.
- When I die (like He died), I will be raised to life again (like He was). Because He rose again, so will I when I'm with Him in heaven. That's when I will get to see all those who have died in faith throughout history. They are alive and together we will "enter into the joy of our Master."

Something amazing happened at daybreak on the morning Jesus rose from the dead. The author of life won the victory over sin. And death lost its power.

The miracle happened again today when someone believes and receives Jesus' gift of eternal life.

Tomorrow: *One on one with Jesus back from the grave*

 Let's talk about it:

1. If someone asked you, "why is Jesus' resurrection such a big deal to you?" What would you say?
2. Which of the three bullet points above speak most to your heart today? "Because Jesus rose from the dead, I can say..."

DAY 30

Mary Magdalene

The One who conquered death

*"Woman, why are you weeping?"
She said to them, "They have taken
away my Lord, and I do not know
where they have laid him." Having
said this, she turned around and
saw Jesus standing, but she did not
know that it was Jesus. Jesus said to
her, "Woman, why are you weeping?
Whom are you seeking?" Supposing
him to be the gardener, she said to
him, "Sir, if you have carried him
away, tell me where you have laid
him, and I will take him away." Jesus
said to her, "Mary." She turned and
said to him in Aramaic, "Rabboni!"
(which means Teacher).* John 20:13-16

She likely had thought of nothing else since Friday night. By
Sunday morning when everyone went back to work, Mary Magdalene
showed up at Jesus's grave, just like she had at every significant event
in His public ministry.

The scene reminds us of why we should adore Mary Magdalene—simply because she was there. Before the navy sky turned purple, then pink and orange. When it was still dark, when her grief had only just begun, she was there.

She had followed Jesus from way back when. Her name tells us she was from Magdala, a town around the lake Jesus called home. It was there Jesus rescued her from seven demons. No telling what kind of shape she was in when they terrorized her soul. When Jesus gave her back her life, she gave her heart to Him in return. She followed Him from that day on.

Everyone needs a witness to their life—someone who knows your history and your stories. Someone who sees both your pain and your progress. In a unique way, Mary and Jesus shared a friendship like that. Jesus stormed through demonic strongholds to rescue Mary and when everyone else ran, Mary stood with Him through the gore and shame of His crucifixion. She had guts and grit and grace. And that's what brought her to His tomb in that pre-dawn. She followed Him to the end.

But it wasn't the end.

Early on that resurrection Sunday morning, when His feet had barely hit the ground again, Jesus stepped out of the shadows to say hi to Mary. The disciples, John and Peter, had come and gone and saw only Jesus' empty grave clothes. Mary lingered behind. Jesus chose her to be the first eyewitness to His new life —and when she didn't recognize Him, all He had to do was say her name . . . *Mary.*

Was the tone of His voice familiar? –the same voice that broke evil's stranglehold on her life not so long ago? *Rabboni! Teacher!* It was her life's truest moment; a tender witness of Jesus' commitment to relationships.

Take a quiet look around at your company of friends. Do you find a Mary? Are you a Mary?—quietly, lovingly, serving the Lord. Perhaps restored from a wrecked past? Committed to the end.

Mary teaches us a lesson in perseverance. Keep at it, all you Marys. The Lord is a witness to your life. He knows your stories. He sees your pain. He delights in your heart, in your love, in your devotion. He who set you free, calls you still to follow. Come discover more about this precious friend you will follow to the end.

Tomorrow: *One on one with Jesus with a faithful doubter*

Let's talk about it:

1. "Take a quiet look around at your company of friends. Do you find a Mary? Are you a Mary?—quietly, lovingly, serving the Lord. Perhaps restored from a wrecked past? Committed to the end." What do you think?
2. Take this to heart, "He knows your stories. He sees your pain. He delights in your heart, in your love, in your devotion. He who set you free, calls you still to follow."

DAY 31

Thomas

The One who proves Himself

Although the doors were locked, Jesus came and stood among them and said, "Peace be with you." Then he said to Thomas, "Put your finger here, and see my hands; and put out your hand, and place it in my side. Do not disbelieve, but believe." Thomas answered him, "My Lord and my God!" Jesus said to him, "Have you believed because you have seen me? Blessed are those who have not seen and yet have believed." John 20:26-29

Christians don't usually set out to doubt God. For most of us, life simply catches us off guard. Hardship trips us up. When we take our questions to God we grow our faith, but we spiral fast when we go solo with our grief.

You can't talk about doubt in Jesus' story without bringing up Thomas. *Doubting Thomas*, people call him. Jesus recruited Thomas along with the other fishermen three years before.

Thomas never lacked commitment. The first time we hear of him, he's rallying the other to follow Jesus to Jerusalem, "Let's go that we may die with Him." Truth is, Thomas will serve Jesus the rest of his life and years from now he *will* die for Him.

Thomas never stopped thinking. He had the guts to raise his hand and ask the Teacher, "Wait. Can you explain that?" Jesus didn't mind. He never had a problem with people with questions—it was people with all the answers who irritated Him.

Thomas didn't have answers. When he heard rumors that Jesus had beat death, Thomas had his doubts, honest ones. After all, he had watched Jesus die last Friday (from a distance). The scene was permanently seared in his memory.

Thomas' signature moment happened a couple days later. He had withdrawn from the others, and struggled in isolation—a dangerous practice for anyone. Doubts only get bigger by yourself.

Jesus, back from death, visited His disciples in the upper room. But Thomas isn't there. So later, all the disciples could do was talk about how Jesus walked through locked doors. But Thomas said, *Sorry guys; I'm just not there yet.* "Unless I put my finger into the nailmarks in His hands, and place my hand into His side, I can't believe."

Thomas wanted to believe; but he had to see Jesus for himself. Eight days later, Jesus showed up again in their hangout—and this time Thomas was there. "Look, Thomas, it's Me. Take your finger and touch my hands. Stick your hand in my side. Don't overthink this, Thomas. Just believe!" (John 20:27)

Thomas didn't have to touch Jesus' nailprints or put his hand in Jesus' side. He gasped, "My Lord and my God!"

"Thomas, because you have seen, you have believed." Jesus said, then added the part about us . . . "Blessed are you, _____, (fill in your name) who has not seen and yet believes." (John 20:29)

Blessed are you reading this now, if you believe. Not, blessed are you if you've never questioned but blessed are you who find in Jesus Christ proof to overcome your doubts. Blessed are <u>you</u>, Jesus says.

Tomorrow: *One on one with Jesus on a Sunday walk*

Let's talk about it:

1. Jesus was kind to Thomas to show up for him in his doubts. How have you experienced doubt about an issue of faith? Has Jesus answered your doubt yet?
2. Why is doubt sometimes good? What best practices have you discovered to take your doubt to a faith-filled conclusion? What can we take-away from Thomas' experience?

DAY 32

Emmaus

The One who changed everything

When he was at table with them, he took the bread and blessed and broke it and gave it to them. And their eyes were opened, and they recognized him. And he vanished from their sight. They said to each other, "Did not our hearts burn within us while he talked to us on the road, while he opened to us the Scriptures?"
Luke 24:30-32

It's Sunday afternoon. A lot has happened in the last 72 hours: Passover. Jesus' trials, His crucifixion, and burial. Sabbath. The death of their dreams.

Two disillusioned disciples leave Jerusalem behind them, along with their hope that Jesus was their Messiah. They pave the road with questions for the next seven miles home, the same way you process something hard as you walk around your neighborhood with a friend. So distracted, they didn't notice the guy who joins them on the sidewalk.

For His own reasons, Jesus keeps them from recognizing Him. "What are you all talking about?" He asks, perhaps with a playful spirit. One of the disciples, Cleopas, says, "Are you the only one in Jerusalem who doesn't know about this?"

Funny. Jesus could have showed up at Pilate's door that afternoon. He could have walked into the Temple and shook the arrogance out of the chief priests who orchestrated His death. A sky full of angels could have announced Jesus' reentry.

Instead, Jesus takes a Sunday walk with two depressed disciples. They believed He was the Christ. That morning, they may have even heard the women returning from Jesus' tomb say, "It's empty!" *Could it be?* Did Jesus rise from the dead like He said He would? If they had believed that, then why are they walking home?

Cleopas and friend walk along, processing their doubts with this stranger. But instead of scolding them, Jesus teaches them. The miles fly by as He opens their eyes to why the Savior had to die. He points them to beautiful pictures of the Messiah throughout the Old Testament.

In Genesis, the Messiah is Father Abraham's ram caught in the bushes. In Exodus, He is the fire by night. In Ruth, He is the Kinsman Redeemer. On through history and through the Law and the prophets, the song of Messiah came to life. As the sun sinks into the horizon, Jesus strings all the notes together for them like a symphony and the disciples recognize the faintest familiar melody playing in their head.

Of course, they didn't want the music to end. When they arrive home, Cleopas invites Jesus to stay the night. It isn't until they sit around the dinner table and Jesus breaks the bread and gives thanks that the whole reality unveils itself in front of them. The Messiah has been with them all along. Perhaps they catch a glimpse of the scars on His wrists, perhaps it is the way He prays for the bread, perhaps Jesus just drops the curtain from their eyes for a moment as He disappeared—who knows except that seeing Jesus changes everything.

Their dinner untouched, the disciples jump from the table and run back to Jerusalem. The mini marathon feels like nothing to them—they are fueled with a message: *Jesus is alive*, people!

Do you know what this means for us today? Jesus walks with us. He talks with us. He's not left us as orphans. Like with the men on the sidewalk home, Jesus gives us enough hope to keep us from giving in to our sadness. Enough of Himself after heartache to help us go on living, go on believing. He has not left us. This changes everything!

Tomorrow: *One on one with Jesus by the lake*

 Let's talk about it:

1. What's your favorite picture of Jesus in the Old Testament? The ram in the thicket in Genesis? The fire by night leading the children of Israel through the desert? The tabernacle? The Shepherd in Psalms?

2. Next time you're discouraged, take a walk around the block and imagine Jesus walks with you. Because He does.

DAY 33

Reunion

The One who made breakfast

Jesus said to them, "Come and have breakfast." Now none of the disciples dared ask him, "Who are you?" They knew it was the Lord. Jesus came and took the bread and gave it to them, and so with the fish. This was now the third time that Jesus was revealed to the disciples after he was raised from the dead. John 21:12-14

Our long look at Jesus' life through the eyes of those He touched is coming to an end. It's a story to keep reading for a lifetime—especially the Gospel of John. The disciple John wrote his gospel nearly 60 years after the events, so "that you may believe Jesus is the Christ, the Son of God, and believing you may have life in His name." Mission accomplished?

As we read John 21 today, you have to wonder if John remembered this last morning around the lake most fondly. You can't miss the nostalgic details: the sunrise on the water. The smell of the fire. His familiar voice. The scars on His wrists. His slight smile at the number of fish reported in the net. His private conversations . . .

These are hinge days—in-between Jesus' resurrection and the beginning of a new season in history. Jesus will return to heaven in a couple days. If success was left up to the disciples, Christianity would have dried up and died in a couple weeks.

But history testifies that's not what happened. The disciples, along with Jesus' mom and brothers, formed the core of 120 people who *could* not and *would* not deny something supernatural happened because of Jesus' life, death, resurrection and ascension. Even better, something supernatural sparked in *them* when they believed He was Messiah, Savior, Lord . . . *God*!

When John remembered that morning with Jesus, you have to wonder if he also recalled the faces of that team around the breakfast fire who each gave his life for Jesus. All of them transformed—one day they were hiding and denying they even knew Jesus—to the next when they ran with the good news to the four corners of the known world.

What happened to them? Just this: God's power filled these uneducated, unsophisticated, insecure followers of Jesus. Because of His Spirit living in them, Acts 17:6 says, "they turned the world upside down."

And the world is still spinning upside down, thanks to Jesus' life working in us today. "Go—tell people about Me," He said as He kicked off the earth a couple days later.

You've heard many one-on-one stories about Jesus. Did you know you have your own story, too? Go write it on the hearts of everyone you meet. Look for opportunities to share history's most amazing true story—and the supernatural thing that's happened to you, too. Ask God to fill You with His Spirit every day, and point you in the direction of people who need Jesus and directions for the way home.

Tomorrow: *One on one with Jesus before lift off*

Let's talk about it:

1. What change have you seen in yourself/others when God's Spirit filled your life?
2. What's your story of Jesus—who is He to you? Practice saying it aloud in as few words as possible. Then don't be surprised when God brings you someone who needs to hear your story.

DAY 34

Homeward

The One who is coming back

Now the eleven disciples went to Galilee, to the mountain to which Jesus had directed them. And when they saw him they worshiped him, but some doubted. And Jesus came and said to them, "All authority in heaven and on earth has been given to me. Go therefore and make disciples of all nations, baptizing them in the name of the Father and of the Son and of the Holy Spirit, teaching them to observe all that I have commanded you. And behold, I am with you always, to the end of the age." Matthew 28:16

When others went home, Jesus went to the Mount of Olives. It was quiet there. The land He loved stretched out like a plaid brown and green blanket tucked around Jerusalem's walls. For all it meant, this hill could have been Jesus' favorite place on earth. Perhaps that's why He took His disciples here to say goodbye.

The Eleven could walk the path blindfolded. Out the East gate, through the ravine, up the incline. They had hiked it with Jesus a few weeks before, the day before He died. Today it felt like old times for them. Jesus, however, had another agenda.

"You're going away?" they whispered. *But you've just come back to us,* they wanted to object.

To identify with this moment, remember how it feels to say goodbye to someone you love. You linger long in the driveway. Hug them again. Talk about the next time you'll be together. When you say, "Goodbye"— you're really saying a shortened, "God be with you." The disciples caught a glimpse of that blessing today on this hill.

"Yes, I'm leaving," Jesus said, "But I'll still be with you."

It's one thing to say God looks down on us from a distance and quite another to say He is with us. Never the detached observer, He promises to be present *in us.* His Spirit connecting with our spirit. His life giving our lives power.

"You will receive power when My Spirit comes upon you," He said pointing east, "You'll tell people about Me here in Jerusalem— then in all Judea and Samaria, and someday to the ends of the earth."

Like on cue, He looked up and His feet lifted off the ground. The clouds swept low and just like that, He was gone. While they still looked up, two men in white clothes appeared beside them, "He's coming back you know; the same way He left. Right to this spot."

In a day before Youtube, the disciples must have replayed that scene in their heads a thousand times. No doubt, they felt homesick watching Jesus disappear into the clouds. But they may also have felt a strange, new feeling of . . . of possibility . . . of hope. *This is not the end.*

Far from it; history tells us it was only the beginning. Before Jesus' instructions will be accomplished, His disciples, then and now, will carry the good news of life in God down a million different roads. It's traveling still, as much through the air now as it has on roads. And Jesus won't touch down again on the Mount of Olives until everyone has had the opportunity to say 'yes' to His offer of life.

As the disciples discovered, this life of faith is full of expectation and adventure—if only because He goes with us. He leads us in Spirit now, until the day He comes back for us in person. Even so come, Lord Jesus.

Tomorrow: *One on one with Jesus for a lifetime*

 Let's talk about it:

1. How have you been aware of God's Spirit at work in your life?

2. How did you first hear the Good News of Jesus? What means of delivery do you use most today? (church, Bible studies, Christian radio, podcasts, websites, YouTube, etc.)

DAY 35

Follow

The One to follow

I count everything as loss because of the surpassing worth of knowing Christ Jesus my Lord. For his sake I have suffered the loss of all things and count them as rubbish, in order that I may gain Christ and be found in him, not having a righteousness of my own that comes from the law, but that which comes through faith in Christ, the righteousness from God that depends on faith—that I may know him and the power of his resurrection, and may share his sufferings, becoming like him in his death, that by any means possible I may attain the resurrection from the dead. Philippians 3:8-11

When you walk with someone for 100 days, you get to know them better. So, how do you know Jesus better now that we've spent this time with Him?

One on one we met the people God used to shape the backdrop of Jesus' arrival as a man on earth. Do you spy the way God worked all things together?

Of course, all of these people and events lead up to these last ones as we walked with Jesus on His way to the cross and the miraculous days following. What did you experience with Jesus during these days?

Did you catch Mary of Bethany's spirit of worship as she cracked open the exquisite vial of oil? Did her mix of grief and love flowing down over Jesus' head touch you, as it touched Him?

Perhaps you meet people like Pilate every day. They are convinced Jesus is more than a man, a good teacher, an icon of spirituality, but for fear of what it will cost are unwilling to enter into a personal relationship with Him.

Or maybe you identify with Nicodemus and Joseph of Arimathea who counted the cost of standing with Jesus—of being His family—and found it to be worth every sacrifice.

We can see ourselves in each encounter with Jesus—in the thief on the cross, in Barabbas, in Thomas.

But of all the lessons and experiences, none could be more meaningful than being with Jesus Himself. What stirred your heart and your faith as you witnessed Him touching us, humbling Himself for us, sacrificing His life for us? That's the real story of these 100 days. He loves us each, one by one. Intentionally. Personally.

His very specific purpose in coming to us is to be our Savior. That's true for His time on earth and it's true today. And it's not just past tense in your life; He's saving you today. He's loving you today. Praying for you today.

These 100 days with Jesus are complete, but how about extending them—just you, one on one with Him, for the rest of your life? That way, on that day when He welcomes you face to face into heaven, you'll know your Savior as your Friend.

May nothing in life be more precious to you than Jesus.

Let's talk about it:

1. What person in Jesus' passion story stands out to you? Who do you identify with?
2. How do you know Jesus better now that you've spent this time with Him?

ABOUT THE AUTHOR

Barb Peil weaves words like invisible threads that helps us build confidence in what we hope for, in things we are certain of, but cannot see. Follow every thread and you'll find Jesus. Follow Jesus and you'll find life.

Barb never expected her life to expand as it has. From early days as one of the first women to graduate from Dallas Seminary to the last 30 years serving behind the scenes in Christian radio, Barb just follows the beauty, surprised at every turn how the evidence unseen always points home. Barb gladly serves today as Vice President of Communications at *Thru the Bible* and lives in Southern California.